A LITTLE BIT OF
LOVE'S MAGIC

BAMBO DEEN

First Published in Great Britain in 2020 by
LOVE AFRICA PRESS
103 Reaver House, 12 East Street, Epsom KT17 1HX
www.loveafricapress.com

LOVE AFRICA
PRESS
African Love Stories

ISBN: 978-1-914226-12-0

Also available in eBook format

DEDICATION

For the women who loved Bewaji and Noura from inception.

BLURB

A young woman finds the person her heart desires with the help of a bit of magic.

Noura is a young I.T. consultant whose weak point is her family. She is at that age when the pressure to get married has hit a new high, but she is not in love with her current boyfriend of three years. After losing a bet, she has to pay a visit to a babalawo in order to obtain a love charm. Despite initial scepticism, Noura follows through with the bet and obtains a charm that is supposed to lead her to true love. The instructions are straightforward, "use this charm and the first person you encounter afterwards will be the love of your life". The only issue is that the first person Noura sees is another   woman.

Bewaji has just moved back to her family home after almost a decade in the United Kingdom. She is looking for nothing more than a haven where she can relax, paint and not think about the row that was the reason she left in the first place. Of course nothing goes as planned, barely a week since Bewaji has returned and her father is trying to play matchmaker. There is also the matter of the gorgeous Noura who seems to believe that she is in love with Bewaji.

4

PROLOGUE

Who had heard of a native doctor living in Ikoyi? Apparently, Gigi had, and that alone was enough to convince Noura that there was little Gigi did not know.

It had all started out as a joke. Rokhaya had got married that afternoon, and the chaos surrounding the wedding was officially over. Noura sat surrounded by friends and family in the upstairs parlour of her mother's house. Now that her younger sister had entered her marital home, inevitably, the topic of her unmarried status came up. As usual, someone had asked about Taofiq and why they were not married yet.

"It's because I don't love him," Noura stated, then took a healthy gulp of red wine from her glass.

Several heads around the room moved left and right, shaking in disapproval.

"That's a weak excuse, Nouratu," her cousin Medina said.

Noura shrugged, silently hoping it would be left at that. Thanks to busybodies like Medina, she felt not only guilty for not only being unmarried but also for not loving her long-time boyfriend.

"Taofiq is such a nice guy," Rokhaya's best lady, Barakat, said. "And the both of you look so good together."

Noura studied the wine swirling in the glass she held. There was just a little bit left, and she downed it.

"If only I loved him," she murmured.

As wonderful as Taofiq was, she could not imagine herself waking up every morning to his face. She had won him over while in her last year at university, and over the years, their relationship had settled into something comfortable. Taofiq liked her, her family loved him, he was also not a jerk, and that was good enough for her.

"Love has little to do with marriage," Medina stated.

"Abeg, leave Noura alone." Older sister Aida wrapped an arm around Noura's shoulders and pulled her in a tight hug.

Just then, Gigi spoke from her corner on the sofa. "What if you loved Taofiq?"

"Huh?" Noura cocked an eyebrow at their long-time family friend.

"I mean, if there was a way for you to love Taofiq. Would you marry him?" Gigi went on. "Because I know a reputable provider of love charms."

A veil of silence settled over the room. One could hear a pin drop before laughter burst forth from all five women.

"Gigi! You are not serious." Medina slapped her thigh as she shook with laughter.

6

"I am very serious o," Gigi insisted, a huge grin on her face. "Noura, think about it. If you don't want these people to know, talk to me in private."

Noura giggled as Gigi winked at her. Just then, Maria entered the room with a newly opened bottle of wine, and the conversation changed focus. As the night wore on, the spotlight turned back to Noura.

"Aunty Noura," Barakat started. "Would you really consider using a love charm on your boyfriend?"

"No," she breathed out. She hated when her younger sister's friends called her "aunty," but she had long grown tired of telling them to stop.

"So you want to be single forever?" Medina's tone was as harsh as her words.

Noura leaned back against the sofa and closed her eyes. Not this again. "I don't want to force anyone to be in love with me."

"Just as it should be," Aida, her all-time supporter, remarked. "You'll fall in love, Noura, and it will be like a slap in the face."

She smirked at her big sister's choice of words. Aida could always be counted on when it came to scoffing in the face of marriage pressure. Medina and Barakat had no idea that she and Aida had been scarred by the memory of Aunty Mulika. Rokhaya was the first of Alhaji Kanjuni's many children to join in marriage even though she was the third-born. Most hope had been lost in the rebellious Aida, but the oversabi generally expected that Noura married first.

"The juju could help facilitate that slap," Barakat joked.

"What if we made a bet?" Medina sat up. "I remember you like bets, Noura."

She groaned. If it would make the marriage-mongers shut up ... "What are the stakes?"

"If you lose this, you'll have to get that love charm ..." Medina's eyes glowed as the gears in her head spun.

CHAPTER ONE

"Gigi, are you sure this is a spa?" Noura asked as Gigi drove past the gates of a mansion and found a suitable space to park.

"Trust me." Gigi's face sported a wide, easy grin. "Let's go."

A young man dressed in all white opened the front door. He then led them to a room and motioned for them to sit down.

"Fatoki will see you shortly," he droned in a sonorous voice before leaving them alone.

"What's that about?"

Noura frowned then shrugged. It was her first week at her new job, and Gigi had surprised her with a spa date to celebrate new beginnings. However, she eyed her friend—from the way Gigi bounced on the chair, she was definitely hiding something.

"I can't hold it in anymore." Gigi trembled. "We are here to get you your love charm."

Noura's nostrils flared. "What?"

"Remember the bet you lost?" Gigi laughed, completely missing the change in Noura's mood. "Don't think you can get out of it so easily."

Of course she had lost the bet. She had failed to correctly guess Rokhaya's honeymoon destination. But that did not matter. She had only agreed to the stupid bet to shut Medina up. She'd had no intention of seeking any love charm. Imagine someone like her visiting a native doctor. Jumbled images of all the Yoruba movies she had watched flashed in her mind. Red cloth on walls, gaudy skull and bones paintings, calabashes filled with orange-tinted sacrifices, a middle-aged man dressed in white probably with some chalk markings on his face and beads around his wrists and neck.

Noura shuddered. She wanted nothing to do with it, and Gigi had tricked her.

"This is ridiculous." She rose to her feet.

She should have seen past Gigi asking her to spend the day. She could have been at home watching the latest episode of her favourite zombie apocalypse series.

"Nouratu." Gigi called her full name.

"I don't need a love charm. Come and take me home."

"Now that we are here, why don't you just see this through?" Gigi changed her tone and became conciliatory. "Are you even listening to me?"

Noura pursed her lips, tapping her foot impatiently against the tiled floor.

She had not noticed it at first, the wall on her left. It touched her subconscious because it took her a while to realise that the wall held an interesting piece of art. The mural's borders resembled ankara print, geometric designs in cool colours, black, blue,

10

and a yellow-brown. In the centre was an oval shape painted black with swirling spots of ochre. Tiny legs projected from this dark shape, looking like an insect crawling somewhere. It was strange, but the more she looked at the mural, the calmer she felt. Her anger slowly faded, and she finally faced her friend.

"If you're uncomfortable, we could go." Gigi pouted. "I got too excited with this, but Baba is really good."

The way the edges of Gigi's lips reached for her chin made Noura smile. "You could have just told me where we were going."

"If I did, would you have come?"

"No," she replied truthfully, but smiled to ease Gigi's blatant discomfort. "But I did go to this so-called Baba's website ..."

"It's nice, isn't it?" Her eyes widened comically.

"It is," she agreed. In her attempt at convincing her to visit this place, Gigi had sent her a link to Fatoki's website. Curiosity had led her to click on the blue line. "I also watched his videos on YouTube."

Despite her scepticism, Fatoki's credentials impressed her. Not only had he lectured in a prestigious university in the UK, he had given lectures around the world in several countries ranging from the US to Brazil, South Africa to Japan. The picture on his website showed a middle-aged man wearing a suit and glasses. He looked more like a political aspirant than a native doctor.

"I wonder how you know him, Gigi." Noura tilted her head and regarded her friend.

Unease flashed across Gigi's face, but it was gone so quickly, she wondered if she had imagined the entire thing.

It must be from her job. Gigi had worked as a researcher in the embassy of a country that was small but rich. Her career brought her in contact with all sorts of individuals.

"I came to get my horoscope read," Gigi responded. "Although it's not really called horoscope here—ah, here he comes."

Noura's head spun, and she saw Fatoki in person for the first time. He looked exactly like his picture except taller than she'd imagined. He wore trousers and over it a plain white shirt in the traditional style. She would have fainted if he'd come out in jeans.

"Baba," Gigi greeted, bending her knees slightly in respect. "This is my friend I was telling you about, Nouratu."

Fatoki stretched his hand out, and Noura regarded it warily. Was she not supposed to kneel down as per tradition?

She took his hand. "Noura. Nice to meet you, sir."

"Your dear friend has told me a lot about you." Fatoki pumped her hand. "It is great to finally meet you."

She did not know how to respond to that, but Baba was not one to waste time.

"You will have to excuse us, Gigi," he said before he led Noura out of the waiting room.

They did not walk far, just to a small study to one side of the hallway. Noura's head was already reeling from the experience. She was really meeting a native doctor in an office. She took a seat opposite Fatoki, a large mahogany desk spanning the space between them.

"Make yourself at ease, Noura."

The fact that he said her name the way she preferred it took her tension down one notch.

She smiled. "This is a lovely ... establishment you have here."

Fatoki returned her smile. He sat opposite her, and she noticed the mural on the wall behind him. Similar to the one in the living room, this painting was all earthly colours, black, brown, ochre with a bit of yellow to brighten the mix. Everything about it seemed traditional, from the motifs that she could not place to the colours.

Fatoki craned his neck to look behind him.

"I see you like my daughter's painting." The pride in his voice rang evident.

"She is an artist?" She could not help the note of surprise in her voice.

"She is." Fatoki's smile was proud. "I am one parent who will not complain when my child draws on my walls."

She snickered, slightly relaxed.

"Baba—" the appellation came surprisingly easy. "—I am sure Gigi has told you about me. I am in a relationship with a man that I do not love."

Fatoki nodded. "She has, but it is better to hear this from you yourself. What exactly do you want?"

"I want to fall in love," she blurted out.

As soon as the words left her mouth, she raised a hand up to her lips.

"There is no need to be ashamed," Fatoki assured her as he rose from his chair.

He walked towards a shelf that resembled those from the Chinese medicine shops she had seen in one of the badly written martial arts movies she loved as a teenager. There were rows and rows of tiny drawers that presumably held things like love charms. Fatoki pulled open one of them, and the smell of traditional black soap slowly filled the room. She recognised that scent and swallowed.

"Do you speak Yoruba?" he asked.

"Yes." She sat up straight as she answered.

"That is good." He took out what looked like a small bar of the soap wrapped in brown paper. "You should be comfortable enough to read the incantation."

Noura bit her lip. She was not sure about that at all. She had always considered incantations to be deeper parts of Yoruba language that she would never need. There, she abruptly stopped her train of thoughts. Wait a minute, who said she was going through with this charm anyway? Visiting the Baba was one thing, but actually using the love charm?

"I will print it out for you." Fatoki returned to his seat. "This is black soap, pounded with something to help you find love."

"Can't I get black soap from anywhere?" she wondered aloud.

To her surprise, he was not upset by the question. "You can get black soap anywhere, but not this special mix, and it would not be complete without the magic words."

"So I am to have a bath, and then what?" She could not help the scepticism that crept into her voice.

"After the spiritual bath, you will meet someone to love." He was unperturbed. "I must warn you that this soap is very potent."

The sound of the printer working jarred the silence in the room. He handed her the sheet of paper.

"These are the magic words."

***

She'd said she could speak Yoruba, not read it. Noura frowned at the piece of paper, at the dots below the 'o's and the accents on the vowels. She easily recognised some words, but others took several pronunciation trials. She sat cross-legged on her bed studying the incantation, the warmth of her mum's dinner still in her belly.

That was one of the advantages of having her mother as a neighbour. When Noura had decided to move out of her father's house, there had been a huge uproar. Her father had been furious, but even at that could not take time out of his busy schedule to reproach her. Rather, it had been Uncle Bola that tried to dissuade her.

When all that had failed, her father and his relatives had gone primal, using her mother as the bad example. That woman was too independent; that woman never submitted to her husband the way she should have; and now, her daughters are following her lead. It was the modus operandi when it came to her extended family—they always badmouthed her mother first, then Aida who was a single mother. After the defaming came the pleas, but Noura had been set in her decision.

After their mother had left their father when he married a second wife, Noura and her sisters had immediately wanted to run away to be with Khaira. Being children, it had not been feasible, so they'd vowed that whenever they got the chance, they would leave their father and stepmother. They romanticised the notion of finding their mother and reconnecting with her. Noura always imagined that when she left her father's house, it would be to her husband's, but having passed the quarter-century mark and making enough money to move out on her own, she'd leapt at the chance.

It was just her luck that she found the perfect boys' quarters with a single bedroom, a quaint parlour, and tiny kitchenette in the same estate her mother lived in. That meant delicious meals and more time spent with her mother than she would have ever hoped for as an adolescent terrified by her mother's departure.

For the tenth time, she tried reading the incantations. She screamed in frustration when the words jumbled across her tongue, and reached for her phone.

"Hey, babes!" Gigi's voice sounded cheery, music thumping in the background.

"Don't babes me," Noura replied. "Come and fix this mess you've put me into."

"Are you referring to the love charm?" Gigi giggled.

"I can't believe I'm considering it." She chewed her bottom lip.

"Yes!" Gigi cheered. "Do it!"

"But the incantations are hard." She let herself fall on her back, her head hitting a pillow.

"Just take them with you to the bathroom, say the words slowly," Gigi advised. "But how are you going to meet the love of your life at this time of the night?"

Noura sighed. "I called Taofiq over."

"Okay ..." Even with the music and the telephone lines, she could still make out the uncertainty in her friend's voice. "Yes, you said you wanted to love him. Sha be careful babes ... ehn?"

She waited as Gigi carried out a conversation on her end.

"Sorry I have to go now." Gigi laughed as though someone was tickling her.

"Say hi to Michael." Noura assumed she was with her latest boyfriend.

"Ah, yes, will do," Gigi answered. "Call me when it works."

Noura let the phone rest on her ear after Gigi had hung up. It was barely nine o'clock on a Friday evening, and Gigi was already out catching fun. Gigi never introduced her to the people she dated, and Noura figured it was because she changed men as often as she washed dirty plates. They were similar in that way, but she had calmed down after Taofiq. She and Gigi were the early bloomers in secondary school, chasing boys and not giving a toss what anyone had to say about it. Aida thought the aggressive boy craze was a coping mechanism Noura developed after the divorce.

Inhaling deeply, she lifted herself off the bed and slipped out of her T-shirt and harem pants on the way to the bathroom. Taofiq would be here any minute. It was time to test that bar of soap.

***

'On my way'

Taofiq had sent that message over an hour ago, and Noura was tired of waiting. She had had the bath, spent a few seconds surprised by how moisturised her skin felt after the black soap, before opting to wear something provocative. As she slipped into the sheer red babydoll she had picked for herself while buying lingerie for Rokhaya's hen party, she'd wondered if sex with Taofiq would be different after she fell in love with him. On a whim, she asked the question to her sister via a text message.

A second later, Aida's reply came. *'What are you talking about?'*

Noura yawned and sat on the edge of her bed. *'I have had my spiritual bath'*

'What? Lol! Rokhaya better not hear of this'

She could picture Aida roaring with laughter. She could also see Rokhaya's disapproving face framed in a colourful hijab.

'Seriously, if I fall in love with Taofiq that's it right?' she typed.

'Having second thoughts?' Aida replied.

'Nope!' If she typed it, maybe she could convince herself. *'How is my baby?'*

'Cheikh is fine and asleep. Do you want me to call?'

The gentle tap on her door caused her to spring off the bed. She hastily wrote a reply to Aida as she rushed the few steps towards the front door.

'Not now, talk tomorrow'

She hit send as she reached to open the door, a reprimand for Taofiq on the tip of her tongue.

A cool night's breeze hit her as the door swung open. Her eyes grew to the size of headlamps when she realised that the person standing before her was not Taofiq. Her lips parted, and she stood still observing this stranger.

She was rooted to the spot, but within her, it was as if a circus had launched a grand performance. Her pulse raced, and her breath quickened; her heart danced to a furious beat while her stomach performed backflips. Further down between her thighs, a forest fire raged, and all of a sudden, her legs could not support her.

She lost her grip on the door as her knees pulled her down towards the ground, but the stranger intervened. That only made things worse. The stranger's hand holding her up burned her waist.

She felt light-headed being this close. Noura stared into eyes framed with long dark lashes and a colour that was red and gold.

Such pretty eyeshadow.

"Are you all right?" The stranger cleared her throat.

Her voice had a slight accent that Noura associated with Great Britain.

Noura willed her legs to cooperate. She tried to stand, but her knees still felt wobbly.

"I am fine." She leaned against the doorframe. "Can I help you?"

This voice was not Noura's. Nouratu's voice was sensible and slightly high-pitched. Who did this raspy, seductive voice belong to?

"You're Noura Kanjuni, right?" The stranger shifted from one foot to the other. "You left your scarf at my dad, Odusina Fatoki's house. He sent me to give it to you, but today has been busy for me. I'm sorry to pass by so late …"

Her lips were moving, but Noura could not really hear her. Instead, she was studying those lips, lips that were full and slathered in a bright orange colour. Her gaze shifted to the long kinky twists that sat on her head in a doughnut and made her face look long and elegant.

Her eyes sought Fatoki's daughter's large ones, which regarded her as she explained why she had stopped by at such an odd hour. Then, her eyes continued their journey, travelling along the length of her neck, appreciating the way the tank top she wore fitted against the curves of her body and the shorts that showed off fleshy thighs.

When Noura's eyes came back up to her face, she noticed Fatoki's daughter staring at her expectantly. Looking down, she saw the outstretched hand holding a silk scarf.

"Than—" Her mouth was filled with saliva she swallowed. "Thank ... you."

"My pleasure." Fatoki's daughter gave a lopsided smile that looked so adorable. "Good night."

As she made to leave, Noura found her voice and called after her. "What is your name?"

"Oh, I am sorry," she apologised. "I'm Bewaji."

"I'm Noura," she breathed. It did not occur to her that Bewaji already knew who she was.

"Nice to meet you, Noura." Bewaji coughed. "Good night."

How can someone be so beautiful? she thought as she watched Bewaji rush towards the front gate.

It was only after the tall figure had disappeared, and the strange feelings her appearance had evoked reduced, that Noura realised she just met a stranger wearing nothing but see-through lingerie.

Soon after that, she noticed that the scarf was not even hers.

CHAPTER TWO

It did not work.

Noura had waited for Taofiq, and he did not show up until the morning after. Things had not gone according to plan. Nonetheless, he was still the first man she had set eyes on following her spiritual bath.

She stared at him while he apologised, giving excuses as to why he had not shown up. She studied his strong face and square jaw that sported a day's-old beard. He wore trousers and a black jalabiya that emphasized his broad shoulders. As he explained why he'd missed their date, he elaborated with his hands and looked at her through half-lidded eyes, licking his lips intermittently.

Yes, Taofiq was good-looking. No, her feelings towards him had not changed at all. It was still the same indifference; the spark just was not there. She considered another bath, especially since he was right there, but then dismissed the thought completely. Clearly, love charms did not work.

"I am so sorry, baby." He pulled her in a tight hug and stroked her back with his large hands.

She stepped out of the hug.

"I waited all night for you," she complained.

"I was at a meeting, I told you." Then his phone started ringing, and he glanced at the screen. "I need to take this call, baby."

She disregarded him as he rushed out the front door and closed it behind him. He would say it was work, but she was sure he was seeing someone else. She wondered why the thought of Taofiq cheating did not really bother her. It must be the lack of love. At this point, their relationship felt more like a contract than anything else.

She continued the weekend cleaning she had started before he arrived. Thirty minutes must have passed before he came back in.

"That was work." He held up his phone. She smiled at her correct estimation of his character. "I am needed urgently."

"Sure." She dragged a damp cloth over the centre table in her parlour.

"Are you still upset with me?" He took her hand and pulled her up to her feet, then wrapped his arms around her waist and held her close once more.

"No, I'm not," she mumbled.

The kiss he gave her before leaving was short and sweet. It also cemented the fact that nothing had changed in her feelings for him.

After cleaning to her satisfaction, she called Gigi to whine. She gave up when her friend did not answer the call. Gigi must be resting after the party the night before. She settled with messaging Aida, the only person other than Gigi who knew of her visit to Fatoki.

'*So nothing changed at all?*' came Aida's message.

'*Nothing*' she replied.

'*Even the sex?*' Aida asked.

'*That didn't even happen*' She groaned as she stuffed a chocolate cream biscuit into her mouth.

'*How do you feel otherwise?*' Aida asked.

She paused to consider Aida's question. Honestly, she felt relieved. In the end, she could not imagine being in love with Taofiq despite his positive qualities.

'*Have you gone out today? Maybe it'll work on someone else?*' Aida added after a lapse of ten minutes.

From her older sister's tardy reply, Noura guessed that her nephew was keeping her occupied.

Someone else. Unheeded, her mind went to Fatoki's daughter. She had thought of Bewaji often since their awkward introduction, but there was no need to mention that to Aida.

'*Doubt that would happen*' She responded.

'*I'm taking Cheikh to a birthday party, want to join us?*' Aida inquired.

She declined the invitation, not feeling like attending a party with rowdy three-year olds even though she loved her nephew. Rather, she decided to see her mother. She slipped on an abaya before making her way to her mother's house. It was a short walk to the duplex. She let herself in through the back door and found her mother in the kitchen liberally pouring wine into a glass.

"*Maman!*" Noura called. She checked her watch—it was not even midday.

"*Ma fille.*" Khaira beamed at her daughter and spread her arms wide. "Come and give me a kiss."

Shaking her head, she walked into her mother's embrace and stifled laughter as she kissed Khaira on both cheeks. The French sensibilities of her mother never failed to amuse her. Khaira had grown up in Togo, the daughter of a successful businessman, and in her youth had made Paris her second home.

"Enjoying wine so early in the morning?" She pointed at the glass.

Khaira raised it in a salute. "Sometimes, a woman has to treat herself. Would you like one?"

She shook her head no, then headed into the sitting room. There were few women who treated themselves like Khaira did. Not only was her mother enjoying wine, she looked like she was going to one owambe even though Noura knew that Khaira may not do more than have a few friends over to gossip later in the day.

"Your sister just left with Cheikh." The silk three-piece Senegalese outfit Khaira wore billowed out around her as she settled on the sofa.

"I know." Noura reached for the remote control and started flipping through the channels.

"Are you hungry? There's jollof rice in the fridge."

"I will eat later. How are things?"

"They are as you left them." Khaira sipped from her glass. "And you? No plans today? I thought you would go with Aida and Cheikh."

"Honestly, mum dearest, I thought I would spend today with Taofiq, but I changed my mind last night." Her eyes were glued to the screen—there was nothing interesting on.

"You're still with that boy?" Khaira remarked as if she did not know.

Noura rolled her eyes. It was not that her mother disliked Taofiq—it was more like Khaira had always been sceptical of the institution of marriage since the fiasco with Alhaji Kanjuni. She saw no point in Noura bowing to the pressure.

"*Maman*, you know I am still with Taofiq." She decided to leave it on an episode of *Come Dine With Me*. "I know you don't like him ..."

There must have been a time when her parents were truly in love. That all changed when ten years into the marriage, her father had chosen to marry another wife. Khaira had been devastated when she found out, but it was nothing compared to her discovery that the second wife had a child the same age as Rokhaya. That was proof that Alhaji Kanjuni's infidelity far outreached his announcement of marrying a second wife.

Things devolved after her dad brought his younger wife to live with them. He grew increasingly hostile towards Khaira, even baring her from leaving the house to go to her shop where she sold gold and precious jewels. Eventually, Khaira could not take anymore. The extended family, the elders, everyone urged her to accede. She was told to be compliant and think of the children—after all, her husband was only being a man. In the end, Khaira got her divorce, but leaving Alhaji Kanjuni came at the cost of losing custody over her children.

It had taken around a decade before they relinked with their mother as adults. When they were younger, their father never allowed it.

"I don't understand." Khaira shook her head. "If your father and his people are saying you must marry, you know I am not among them."

"I know." Noura smiled at her mother.

***

The next time Noura went to Fatoki's house, she was alone. She was here to inform him that what he had given her did not work after Gigi's insistence. Or so she told herself. If she admitted the truth, she wanted to see Fatoki's daughter again. Even through the ups and downs that came with her job as a UX designer moonlighting as a project manager, she could not stop thinking about that encounter.

Sometimes, it felt like she had imagined it all. At the most inappropriate situations, she would vividly remember the way she felt that night, and all of a sudden, she would start trembling. Sitting through meetings with the clients and briefing them about progress so far in the sprint, she would recall the red-gold of Bewaji's eye shadow, and that would be enough to render her inarticulate. Skin flushed, she would stutter her way through focus groups and lab testing sessions after the image of Bewaji's face drifted through her mind.

Slamming the door of her car, she headed towards the front door and pressed the bell. The first time, she and Gigi did not have to wait long for someone to answer. However, this time was different. Noura pushed the button again; there had to be someone at home. She looked over her shoulder. Surely, the security guard would not have let her in if no one was home.

Hearing the door open, she turned, and warmth flooded through her as she recognised Bewaji. Noura did not mean to, but her eyes scanned Bewaji's visage.

"Hello, Bewaji." Her lips parted. "Is your father around?"

Today, Bewaji wore no makeup, a white tank top, and shorts. In defiance of the simplicity, her face glowed. It was incredible to Noura.

"No, he is not." Bewaji frowned.

Noura could not help the crestfallen expression that graced her face—she was disappointed. Now, she had no reason to cross the threshold.

"Um ... he should be back soon," Bewaji rushed to add. "Do you want to wait for him?"

"I would love to wait for him." Noura beamed.

She let Bewaji lead her into the house. They walked down a hallway, and she noticed Bewaji was taking her to the same room she and Gigi had waited in before. That was not what she'd expected, but she decided to bide her time and sat down on the same chair as before.

"Can I get you something to drink?" Bewaji tossed thick braids over her shoulder, the move exposing the butterscotch of her rounded shoulder.

Noura stared at her. It took a while for Bewaji's question to penetrate her consciousness. "Yes, please," she breathed. "Some water."

Bewaji's hips swayed as she walked out of the room. All of a sudden, the prospect of waiting alone seemed glum, and Noura shot up from the chair.

"Hold on," she called out to that back. Bewaji looked over her shoulder, and Noura held back a gasp. "If you don't mind, can I wait with you?"

She twisted her fingers as Bewaji regarded her.

"I mean, it would be boring to wait here on my own." As soon as the words left her mouth, she cringed inwardly. Could she have sounded any more desperate?

Bewaji's small smile caught her unawares, making her feel instantly lighter.

"I don't mind, Noura."

The way she said her name raised goose bumps along her skin.

Leaving her handbag behind, she followed Bewaji through to the kitchen. She leaned against the cool tiles of the kitchen wall, seeking respite from the heat that suffused her. She did not understand why she could not take her eyes off Bewaji.

There should be nothing sensual about rinsing a glass with water at the sink, but the water gliding off Bewaji's smooth hands entranced her. Her fingers tingled with the need to see if Bewaji's skin was as velvety as it seemed. These sensations would have confused her if she stopped to really think about what she was feeling. She swallowed, not knowing what was going on, but it felt good.

"Here."

Bewaji offered the water, startling her from her reverie. Her hands shook as she accepted the glass.

She thanked the other woman and drank the water, hoping it would dampen the fire raging inside her.

Then she remembered part of the reason she had come here in the first place.

"The scarf you gave me is not mine."

"Really?" Bewaji asked, her head tilted to the side. "Dad was pretty certain it was."

There was an awkward silence during which Noura turned the glass in her hands over and over again.

"Are you the artist?" she blurted out.

Bewaji's head jerked back in surprise. "Yes, I am."

"Your father told me about you." Again, she did not like her choice of words after she had said them, but she continued. "You painted the mural in the waiting room, too."

Bewaji nodded. "Are you interested in the arts?"

"Very much so," she replied earnestly. She could not draw a stick figure, but she appreciated fine art. "You need to tell me what message you were trying to convey in that mural."

"The one in the waiting room shows a dung beetle." There was a small smile on Bewaji's face. "It is supposed to symbolise patience."

Is that why looking at it calmed me down? she thought while staring at Bewaji with wide eyes and raised eyebrows. So this was the artist daughter

Fatoki was so proud of. She appreciated that her talking about art seemed to ease the tension in the room.

"I was painting before you came, if you are interested—" Bewaji offered.

"Of course!" she replied without waiting for her to complete her sentence.

This time, she kept her eyes averted when Bewaji led the way to the dining room just next-door. She was immediately drawn to the work in progress, evident by the tins of opened paint and the stepladder before it. Everything else in the room had been pushed to one side so the space around the mural was free. Noura observed what seemed to be a pile of pots tilting precariously on the far right of the painting. It was silly that to her the pots did not look like cooking utensils at all—rather, their shape brought to mind the figure of a well-endowed woman.

"What does this signify?" she found herself asking.

Bewaji rubbed the back of her neck with a hand. "I am not sure how to explain it."

"It looks like there are stars in the pots." She moved closer to the wall to investigate the yellow swirls of light in the dark pots.

"Well—" Bewaji began, the doorbell ringing, stopping her short. Her eyes travelled to the apple-shaped clock on the opposite wall.

"Oh, wow, it's two already? She's early for the first time," she muttered more to herself, but Noura heard every word. "Excuse me."

Bewaji rushed out of the room. Noura bit her lip, wondering who this 'she' interrupting her and Bewaji's time was. She gulped down the cold water, emptying the glass. There was a high-pitched squeal that she heard easily even though the dining room was quite a distance from the front door. She could make out the chatter before Bewaji re-appeared with a woman. Noura noticed their entwined hands.

Who held hands out of secondary school? she thought as she waited for an introduction.

"Baby girl, this is Noura." Bewaji motioned towards her. "Noura, this is Ubeyi."

"Nice to meet you." Noura waved at Ubeyi, lips pursed.

Ubeyi stood shorter than Bewaji, her wavy Peruvian weave reaching bra-length and curled at the ends. Her face was expertly made up, eyebrows drawn in a perfect arch and lips a pink pout.

She found herself wondering if Bewaji called all her friends 'baby girl' and held their hand like that. As Ubeyi greeted her back, she was filled with the sudden urge to leave.

"I should be on my way," she announced.

"Have you given up on waiting for my dad?" Bewaji stopped her.

She bobbed her head.

"I'll just come back. I should have made an appointment first. Don't worry." She stopped Bewaji from escorting her to the door. "I can let myself out. Have fun with your friend."

When she reached the kitchen, she paused and twirled on her heel, then rushed back to the dining room.

"I was wondering," she asked Bewaji. "Is it okay if I have your number?"

***

"So is that your new catch?" Ubeyi asked, arms crossed under her breasts and eyebrows raised. She had watched closely as they exchanged numbers before Noura scuttled out the room.

Bewaji rolled her eyes.

"I haven't been here long enough." She shrugged. "Besides, I am not looking for anything now."

"That's what they all say." Ubeyi rolled her eyes, too, and leaned against the dining table. "She is fine sha."

"And as straight as a ruler." Bewaji turned her attention to her mural, and with a pang, realised she might not be able to complete it today as planned. It was hopeless to work in front of Ubeyi. Her secondary school friend would keep her distracted.

"Are you interested in her?" She tried to keep her voice flat as she hopped on the dining table next to Ubeyi. Then she helped herself to the bottle of fresh juice her friend had brought with her.

"Abeg don't finish my juice, I am on a juice fast," Ubeyi warned while making no effort to snatch the bottle from her hands. "Plus you know I am happily married."

Bewaji smiled. They had come a long way from cuddling each other on the top bunk. She had been a few months shy of her thirteenth birthday when she'd realised that what she felt for her best friend Ubeyi was more than just 'like.'

But even after their shared kisses and curious explorations, she had convinced herself that it was a phase and nothing serious. The greater part of her never expected to still find women attractive after graduation. Yet, here she was; here they both were. Ubeyi now lived in Ajah with a wife and a kid they were raising together. Bewaji would never have pictured the possibility of that future, especially in Nigeria.

"How are they?" She sipped at the orange-coloured juice, able to taste carrots and ginger.

"Loreen and Amara are great." Ubeyi looked through her phone. "Amara started school last week, you need to see her in uniform."

They oohed over pictures of Amara dressed in a pinafore and holding a backpack. Then Ubeyi scrolled right to a photo of her and Loreen standing next to a round-faced man.

"That's Danjuma," she explained. "The guy you have been talking to. Which reminds me, how far with the job?"

"I am almost done with the sketches," Bewaji responded. It was nice to put a face to the man she had been exchanging emails with for weeks over a commission. She had expected him to be older.

Danjuma and Loreen were close to opening a restaurant—they had the property and almost everything set up. Their vision was to create a literary space that would serve coffee and tea, pastries and light food. Ubeyi had managed to convince them to let Bewaji paint their walls—they bought the idea that unique murals would add to the artsy vibe they had in mind for the place. Apparently, Loreen had hired local woodworkers to carve tables and chairs that would adorn the establishment, too.

"I am sure you'll be excellent since you have the African feel they want so much," Ubeyi cheered. "DJ is obsessed with the photos on your website."

Bewaji could not stop beaming. "I have a meeting with him next week."

"Bewaji the artist!" Ubeyi gave her a playful shove.

A throat clearing interrupted their laughter. She looked up to see her father in the kitchen, peeking through the open door at them in the dining room.

"Welcome back, sir," she greeted. "You remember my friend Ubeyi?"

Fatoki looked at Ubeyi and frowned, trying to recall the face.

"Ah-ah, is this not Titi?" He used Ubeyi's Yoruba name, given to her as she was born and bred in Ijesha.

"Yes, sir." Ubeyi knelt down to greet her father in a way that greatly pleased the traditionalist in Fatoki.

Bewaji, on the other hand, narrowed her eyes. It had always amazed her that her father seemed not to suspect anything untoward between her and Ubeyi. All the summers they spent in her room experimenting, Ubeyi had made a lot of noise with her loud moans.

However, Fatoki warmly asked Ubeyi about her welfare and even patted her on the shoulder. That slight pat was the highest sign of affection for a man who greatly disliked unnecessary body contact. Bewaji had never known a Nigerian man who disliked hugs.

CHAPTER THREE

Bewaji stepped into the garden. The heels of her shoes sank into the damp earth, and the most inappropriate thought crossed her mind. It was of Noura, the only woman she now knew of in real life who opened the front door wearing lingerie.

That gift was surely not intended for her. Nonetheless, the image was still engraved in her mind. She could still picture the swell of Noura's breasts, the multiple strings of beads that adorned where the slim curve of her waist flared out to her hips. She pictured the way Noura's eyes had turned into inviting pools of honey when they met hers. It confused her, but she had more pressing matters at hand.

Shaking her head, she wiped the image but only temporarily. She spotted Danjuma sitting next to a jacaranda tree.

"Good afternoon," she called out.

Danjuma rose to his feet on seeing her and gripped her hand in a firm handshake.

"It is great to finally meet you, Bewaji."

"Likewise, Danjuma." She looked up at the heavyset man, also tall to boot.

"Call me DJ." He motioned for her to take a seat opposite him.

The restaurant he had selected for their first face-to-face meeting was secluded, and their table in the garden even more so. She had to push back the leafy branch of a shrub before settling on the chair.

"Do you want anything?" He signalled to the waiter. A half-empty bottle of whiskey sat in front of him.

"Just water, thanks." She put her backpack on the grass near her chair.

"I must say from what I've seen on your website, your work is impressive," he said.

"Thank you." She preened under the praise. It turned out painting murals at home was a step in the right direction, after all. She had searched ambitiously for clients and had almost forgotten that a well-built portfolio was equally important.

"Loreen and I both agree that your murals will bring the kind of unique atmosphere we are looking for," he continued. "Apologies that she could not make it for this meeting, by the way."

It was fine for her either way as the person she communicated with largely was Danjuma. She also had no complaints with the prompt way they had capitulated to her demands and paid for the sketches beforehand. The issue of her fifty percent upfront payment remained unsettled nonetheless.

"Let me show you the sketches." She was not one to beat about the bush.

DJ rubbed his hands together as she brought out her sketchbook from her bag. When she painted on her own, she painted at will with flexibility. Yet with clients, there was the need to adhere to any specifications and to draw sketches beforehand.

It had been a fun challenge coming up with concepts based on DJ's preferences. In keeping with the overall theme of the establishment, he and Loreen had picked themes from Nigerian folklore. They had commissioned two murals, one on the forbidden forest and another on brave huntresses. Bewaji had drawn two sketches per idea and presently showed them to him.

"Nice," he commented, looking through the sketches.

She stiffened. "Just nice?"

She had put a lot of work into those designs, and the thought of losing her first major client here after becoming invested was shattering.

"If you have any objections or suggestions, I can make changes," she rushed to add.

"At an additional cost?" Then he laughed before she could object. "I am just thinking, this looks excellent on paper, but will it translate? There's a lot of detail in them."

"It will look even better on your walls, I can assure you," she insisted. "The details mean it may take a bit longer to finish these murals, and since I will be working on my own ..."

"Let's start with just one." He stroked his chin and looked through at the four sketches on the table in front of him. "This one."

She took the chosen sketch and smiled—she got to work on the forbidden forest.

"You are quite talented," he started, then paused as a waiter placed a plate containing fries and a burger in front of him. "Loreen likes you, and as far as she is concerned, we must use your services."

"And what do you feel on the matter?" She watched the waiter unscrew the cap from a bottle of water and thanked him after he filled her glass.

"Well, we've already paid for this—" he lifted one of the sketches, "—not to mention we have a budget for decorations. Your art is more interesting than recycled chandeliers."

"I promise I will not disappoint you," she assured him.

"When can you start?" He began picking at his food.

"Immediately." She cleared her throat before broaching the yet unsettled payment. "And this is why I need an initial payment to buy the supplies and set things up."

He waved his hand. "I will transfer the payment to your account right now. Let's see what you can do."

Bewaji swung her arms as she walked out of the garden. The thought of driving around town lugging pots of paint did not deter her. On a whim, she reached into her backpack for her phone. There was a text message waiting to be read. She had a feeling who it was from before she opened the message, and her smile grew even wider when she saw that she was right.

'Hello Bewaji, this is Noura. Very random but did you know that the sign of peace is apparently a broken cross?'

It had taken her long enough to get in touch. She had often thought of making the first move but had held back.

'I have no idea' She sent her reply, then laughed when Noura's message came in.

'I just asked this man to take part in my study on subscriptions oh, next thing he's telling me that the peace sign is from the devil and the end of days are coming'

'Why are you doing a study on subscriptions?' Bewaji asked.

'Part of the job description, guerrilla studies'

Noura's response was as instant as the network allowed.

The texts were rapidly exchanged, flying back and forth through the way home. By the time Bewaji entered through the front door, she had agreed to meet Noura at a gallery the day after next.

***

Kevin placed the crown that was the hairdryer over Noura's head after covering her ears with protection.

"It will need a couple of minutes to dry." He raised his voice over the noise of the dryer.

"How many minutes?" she asked, and laughed when he only assured that it would not be long.

Shifting in the worn leather chair, she kept herself busy with her phone. In the few minutes that had passed while he washed her hair, twenty messages had come through. They were all from her and her sisters' chat group. The trending topic was Rokhaya's honeymoon in the Maldives.

Noura looked through the photos of her sister and Teslim on the beach. Today, their daily excursion had taken them to an ancient mosque built in the seventeenth century. Rokhaya seemed over the moon and sincerely happy that just looking at the sunny photos made Noura smile and wish she were on an exotic island. She took her time responding, praising her sister for looking good after such an extended honeymoon. Soon, the conversation veered to her.

'*How are we preparing for the day off tomorrow big sis?*' Rokhaya asked.

Noura liked her new job a lot. Barely two weeks in and she was already enjoying a random day off. She was looking forward to a long weekend, but this Friday felt even more special.

'*She's making herself pretty for Taofiq*' Aida answered on her behalf.

However, she had no intention of meeting her boyfriend and told her sisters as much.

'*I am going to this gallery with a friend*' She wrote and waited for the reactions.

'*I have work tomorrow and I'm sure Gigi does too, Rokhaya is not in the country...*' Aida replied, in reference to the closed-circuit life Noura lived. They all knew she did not really have many friends outside both of them and Gigi.

'*A friend I just met*' She replied.

'*Hmm, is this friend a "he" or a "she"?*' Rokhaya asked.

Noura rolled her eyes as she replied.

'*A she, really?*' Rokhaya typed. '*You're spending hours in the salon to meet up with a female friend.*'

'*So?*'

She felt herself getting defensive. She had rushed to her usual hairdressers immediately after work, for the first time making use of its twenty-four-hour service. She decided to go drastic—she'd not only cut her hair short but also dyed it.

Kevin had been reluctant, but she had pushed. After growing her natural hair for three years, she could not wait to be reunited with her teeny-weeny afro.

'*The woman just wants to look good*' Aida defused the situation.

'*Exactly*' She added. '*You will all be shocked when you see me*'

She felt she might as well be meeting a 'he' from the way she anticipated the gallery visit, but she had never been this excited about meeting anyone, period. It felt like someone had popped open a tightly corked bottle of joy inside her belly. She was giddy thinking about Friday—she had been looking forward to it since Wednesday when she had asked Bewaji out.

She wondered what Bewaji would think of her haircut. She had even selected the outfit she would wear. She thought she looked sexy yet casual in the knee-length tunic dress made with the age-old Angelina fabric.

The next day, she woke up with a song in her head. She played Ebo Taylor loud and on repeat and danced as she made toast for breakfast, then as she had a shower. Her eyes constantly went to her phone, and she counted down the hours until she could head out to the gallery.

Bewaji only had time to meet in the afternoon, and Noura was good to go by nine a.m. Her body thrummed with energy, but she made herself sit before the TV and watch a French horror movie that was on her list of films to watch. As the ending credits rolled, she put on light makeup and left her apartment.

She drove into the compound that housed the gallery early and met her friend, the manager, at the entrance. Uche took her through to see the newest additions, and later upstairs to his office where he made her listen to his newly acquired vinyl records.

Eventually, the moment she had been waiting for came—her phone vibrated in her purse. Her pulse quickened when she saw Bewaji's name on the screen. Her voice came out smoky when she answered hello.

"Hi, Noura." It felt good to hear Bewaji's voice after days of chatting. "I am at the gallery. Are you here yet?"

"Yes, I am upstairs. Come in, I'll meet you down."

After bidding a quick goodbye to Uche, she rushed towards the stairs. She asked no questions as to what pushed her forward in this manner. All she knew was that she really wanted to see Bewaji again.

She caught a glimpse of her at the landing of the stairs. Of course, the woman looked resplendent enough that her breath caught in her throat. Bewaji wore a grey asymmetrical dress, her long kinky twists let down, and today, her eye shadow was green and gold, her lipstick golden, too.

They stared at each other, seemingly forgetting that a world existed outside the both of them. A sudden shyness overcame her.

"Wait for me jo!" Someone rushed up the stairs, heels clicking against marble.

Noura's joy plummeted as she realised Bewaji was not alone. It must have shown on her face because Ubeyi's smile was viciously wide when she spied Noura.

"Hey!" Her voice was overly shrill. Ubeyi bounded up the final set of stairs, leaving Bewaji behind. "Good to see you again, Noura. This place is amazing."

Bewaji trailed behind looking less excited. Noura wore a pinched expression, a wide variety of thoughts running through her mind. Foremost was why she felt so disappointed that Bewaji had not come here alone. She forced a smile on her face when Bewaji approached her.

"Hello," she mumbled. "Thanks for coming."

She walked behind Ubeyi and Bewaji, chewing the corner of her lips. What she was feeling did not make any sense. There was no reason for her to feel so down that Bewaji had brought that Ubeyi along.

Someone who did not know Noura would say she was jealous.

She shook her head sharply—it was not like this was a date. She dismissed that ridiculous thought from her mind as she went through the motions of introducing Ubeyi and Bewaji to Uche.

She only wanted to know Bewaji more, she reasoned. She wanted to be friends with her. Who would not want to be in the company of someone so gorgeous and who radiated such warmth? Even standing beside Bewaji, who remained silent while her friend chatted with Uche, Noura felt it. She decided to stray away from the two friends and sought the comfort of her favourite painting.

***

Bewaji's eyes hunted for Noura. While Noura regarded the painting, she locked on her. She knew she had not imagined the way Noura's eyes had lit up when she saw her, or the way they'd dimmed upon Ubeyi's appearance. She presently felt her friend tugging at her right arm.

"See, you're interested." Ubeyi clapped her hands, drawing attention from the other visitors. She leaned closer to Bewaji and whispered, "It seems she is interested, too. I say go for it, I'll support you."

She gave a long, low sigh and turned to regard Ubeyi. "Was your plan to make her jealous?"

"Did you see the way her face dropped when she saw me?" Ubeyi's laugh was boisterous. "Now we are clear that madam 'straight' has the hots for you. Remember your promise?"

Bewaji rolled her eyes, but Ubeyi started poking at her ribs, making her jump until she said out loud, "I will give it a chance."

"Excellent." Ubeyi beamed. "Now I have done enough damage. Better go and enjoy your date."

She placed emphasis on the last word and tapped Bewaji's bum as she hurried away. Bewaji's brows crinkled, but her shoulders shook with a quiet laughter. When she hadn't truly known what to make of Noura's invitation, Ubeyi had been over the moon with glee on her behalf.

Her eyes sought Noura again—she was still in front of a painting. The woman looked good with the short hair, and she noticed she had switched her nose ring. Squaring her shoulders, she approached her.

"It's beautiful," she said, drawing Noura's attention.

Noura jumped a little, then almost immediately, her eyes went searching for someone. Most likely Ubeyi, she guessed.

"Are those spaceships?" she blurted, drawing closer to examine the piece of art.

"What are?" Noura asked, looking back at the painting.

She pointed. The painting rendered a woman surrounded by children in geometric shapes. Above the woman and the children were discs that resembled flying saucers. A reluctant smile lit Noura's face.

"I thought I was the only one who noticed the spaceships," she remarked.

"But they do look like UFOs." She basked in Noura's smile. "There is something futuristic about this."

"Do you like science fiction?" Noura asked.

"Are you joking?" Bewaji's eyes widened. "I am re-watching *Stargate SG-1* right now."

"That is awesome." Noura sounded impressed. "I met the artist, and she insisted that those were not spaceships, that they represent the emotion caused by the burdens placed on the woman and the children in her care."

"We both know they are spaceships." She winked.

"Speaking of symbolism—" Noura's eyes widened. "—that reminds me, you never got the chance to tell me what the pots in your work-in-progress signifies."

There was a flutter in her belly. Was Noura really this interested in her?

"With that—" she explained, "—I want to portray a sense of bursting, like something kept tight under a lid that wants to come out. Something that will come out no matter what. I painted stars in the water pots to show that stars could not be kept hidden."

"That is absolutely amazing." Noura's hand was on her heart.

"Thank you." She smiled at her and held her gaze until Noura broke it.

"How goes your contract?" Noura changed the topic. She moved away from the painting to one of the carved wooden stools that were not just breath-taking pieces of art but also made for sitting.

"It is going great. I will start work soon." She was oddly pleased that Noura had remembered their conversation on her work.

The other stools were occupied, so Noura shifted over, creating space for Bewaji to share the seat with her. She was instantly aware of Noura's closeness, the coconut scent of her hair filling her nostrils.

"You look beautiful." She sighed. "Your haircut really suits you."

Noura's hand immediately went to her hair, and she played with the soft coils near her ear. "Thanks."

"How goes your website? Are you still interviewing funny people?"

Noura groaned. "Luckily, I have not met anyone else who sees the devil in everything."

The conversation flowed easily between them, and when it lulled, it came with a comfortable silence. The gallery had given up its gifts, but neither was ready to leave. Bewaji was relieved when Noura suggested a walk.

***

A calm evening draft blew over the Lekki-Ikoyi bridge. Noura had suggested the walk impromptu, but Bewaji was enjoying it tremendously. This was what she wanted. And Noura content enough just listening to her tell her about life as a native doctor's daughter.

When people found out that her father was an initiated native doctor, they usually had one of two reactions: fear or curiosity. She regaled her with stories of fellow students at secondary school demanding that she ask her father for strong juju to pass exams to those at university in London who wanted to see African black magic.

She also knew there were those who believed people like her father to be in league with the devil, too. But to her, her father was simply that. A supporting and loving father who had always done his best for his children even after their mother passed away and his children turned their back on his treasured traditions. She opened up more than she had intended and let details of her time in London slip.

"I just cannot imagine you as an insurance banker." Noura laughed.

They walked close to each other, brushing shoulders, soft skin against skin before moving apart only to be drawn back again.

"Believe it or not." Noura's laughter infected her.

"So why did you come back?"

Her brow immediately wrinkled. Until her brother stumbled upon her sketchbook and found images he considered inappropriate, she had been happy to share the house with him and their sister. Kehinde had not just invaded her privacy, he had then called in Taiwo, and both of them had thought to lecture her over what she drew in private.

Her art was always more symbolic than literal, but it was easy for Kehinde to see that couched in the drawing of a double gong were two women entwined in a passionate embrace. He had been appalled, and Taiwo just as much. Her twin siblings were older than her by almost a decade. In some ways, they raised her and perhaps still thought they could control her. They had followed on their threats to kick her out of the house—she had had to sleep on a friend's sofa while she rounded up her Fine Arts degree. Eventually, she'd decided to come back home to Nigeria.

Despite the years of on-and-off communication, she had been welcomed with open arms. She'd found her father living in a mansion alone except for the occasional acolytes he trained in the worship of the deities and an old cook, Iya Gbenga.

Religion had torn the family apart, yet in her father, Bewaji found a lot of tolerance, more than she had given him credit for in all those years. He supported her artistic aspirations, even offering to pay her to paint on his walls. Her spirit lifted every time Fatoki introduced her to his friends and clients as "my daughter, the artist." She did not want to pull at the limits of her imagination, but she thought her father would not have minded if he had been the one to find that sketch.

It was taking her too long to answer, and Noura noticed.

"You do not have to answer if it's uncomfortable," she said.

"No, I want to tell you." Bewaji inhaled, her hand reaching up to play with a twisted strand of hair. She would tell Noura part of the truth. "I fell out with my siblings."

"Oh."

"My older siblings are very opinionated," she continued. "And I always followed their lead. I do not mind that Dad is a traditional priest, but they thought it was sinful, so I eventually thought the same, too. Part of the reason I was able to get that job with that bank is because my sister Taiwo had worked there before. I thought they wanted the best of me, but there are ... parts of me that they do not like."

That was as much as she would reveal, yet she felt like the burden had been lifted off her shoulders. When Noura's supple hand reached for her own, the anxiety within her lessened even more.

"It was either stay and fight, or leave and be happy." She gave a small, sad smile. "Besides, I got to reconnect with Dad. It's been seven years."

Their pace had slowed, and eventually, both women stopped.

"I am so sorry," Noura said, still holding onto her hand.

"It's alright." She squeezed Noura's hand. "I didn't mean to spoil the mood, but it is so easy talking to you."

***

Noura observed Bewaji. She looked pained at the quarrel with her siblings; anyone would be. She silently prayed that their relationship would be mended.

"Look, look!" Bewaji said excitedly as if she would miss something.

She lifted her brows and turned, confused, but then, she saw it.

A scene she had hardly noticed or appreciated in the busy life she led: the sun was setting. A dull orange behind dark blue clouds, this was nature's art. A volcano in her centre slowly let off some steam. The next time she peeked at Bewaji, she saw that the woman was looking at her.

This is so romantic, she thought, then stamped that impression out as one would hit a cockroach with a shoe. It would be romantic if she were here with a man she was romantically involved in, and Bewaji was just a friend.

Yet, their eyes forged a connection that could not easily be broken. How had they come so close? She noticed Bewaji's long lashes; she felt Bewaji's breath on the bridge of her nose. Was Bewaji's face moving closer? She did not move away.

A speeding car blaring its horn tore the moment apart. She leapt back as though shocked by an electric current, and in the process let go of Bewaji's hand.

Was she about to kiss Bewaji a moment ago?

She brought a hand to her lips. No, that was not it, she reasoned, or tried to 'til she decided that she was not going to think about it and attempted to shelve the memory. She was enjoying this time and would not spoil it.

They watched the sun set together and stayed until darkness fell and the bridge lit up.

CHAPTER FOUR

The cafe was cosy and busy in the evening. Noura waited for her caramel Frappuccino and Bewaji's iced black coffee. Bewaji had excused herself earlier to use the bathroom while she protected their seats. She had to have only been gone for five minutes, but already she missed her company.

How come she felt so at peace in a relative stranger's company? Despite living in the same house as them while growing up, she still felt discomfort when she had to spend long amounts of time with her father or her stepmother. Yet, someone she had met just—she counted—three times was making her want to spill out her soul. Her cheeks even hurt from smiling, but she loved this pain. It was not forced; with Bewaji, everything felt so laidback.

She knew nothing much would come from an over analysis and pushed this feeling into the already bulging mental box where she stored things she did not want to think about right now.

Unbidden, her mind flitted back to the bridge. Bewaji's face had been so close to hers. What was happening there? Did Bewaji want to kiss her? Why would Bewaji want to? But wait, would she mind if Bewaji kissed her?

Noura's cheeks heated as she found herself wondering if Bewaji's lips would be as soft as they looked. How would they feel against hers? She cupped her cheeks with both hands. But what on earth was she thinking? She slapped her hand on her forehead just as the waiter brought their drinks. He must have thought she was mad, but she gave him a huge smile as she thanked him.

That would be a first, if Bewaji kissed her. If asked, she would say she had never kissed a girl before. Yet, there was that one time in primary school where the spun bottle had pointed its spout at her and its end at a family friend whose name she could not remember. She could however recall that the girl smelled strongly of sweat and that she had felt nothing then.

"Ra-ra!"

She could pinpoint Aida's voice even in the midst of a storm, and Aida used that annoying nickname, too. It was a relic of their childhood, when she and her sisters gave themselves nicknames by doubling the last syllable of their names. Ra-ra, Ya-ya, of course Aida hated hers the most because it became Da-da, so she went for Ai.

Noura's head spun in search of her sister, and soon, Aida pushed through the crowd and came into view, Cheikh in one hand and a paper bag stained with the butter of the treats it contained in the other.

"Ai, what are you doing here?" she asked stupidly.

Aida only had a warm smile and a hug. "Our baby wants a muffin."

"Aunty Ra-ra," her little nephew called for her, stretching out his small hands. Noura lifted him in a tight hug, but her mind was not there.

"How are you, my baby?" she asked, tickling his tummy.

"Fancy bumping into you here," Aida chimed. "Is your friend around? Or did you leave her in the gallery?"

Aida's sharp eyes had already scanned the table Noura was seated at alone and noticed the two drinks. Noura wanted to hide the iced coffee. For some reason, the idea of Aida seeing Bewaji put her in panic mode. It was unreasonable, she knew, yet her sister knew her so well, so she started blabbing.

"What? No!" she protested. "I mean yes, yes, I did."

"You are doing that thing you do when you are nervous." Aida's eyes narrowed. "Are you sure this your friend is a she?"

From behind her sister, she glimpsed Bewaji making her way slowly towards the table.

"... because you know I won't judge you if you are cheating on Taofiq," Aida went on.

"I am not cheating on Taofiq," she hissed.

"So why are you acting ..." Aida's tone was uncertain.

Bewaji reached the table and smiled at Noura while waiting for introductions, but Noura was trying to get Aida to leave.

"I am here with a friend." She held her sister's arm and whispered, "Don't make a big deal out of this."

Aida eyed her and shrugged off her hand. "I would say you are the one making a big deal, what is wrong with you?"

She turned to Bewaji and introduced herself in a ringing tone.

"Hello there." Aida took Bewaji's hand in a handshake. "I am Aida, Noura's sister, and that adorable ball of sunshine is Cheikh. My sister has clearly forgotten her manners."

Bewaji eased the lips she had squeezed tightly. "I am Bewaji. Hello, Cheikh."

She waved at the boy who hid his face in the crook of Noura's neck.

"Do you want to sit down with us?" Bewaji asked.

"No," Noura answered firmly. "Aida will be going now."

Both Aida and Bewaji looked at her as if she had sprouted an extra pair of eyes. And maybe she had. It made no sense even to her that she should not want Bewaji to meet her sister, but she went along with the instinct.

"Okay." Aida pursed her lips. "Come here, Cheikh. Your Aunty Ra-ra wants us to leave."

As Aida took Cheikh from her arms, Noura whispered in her ear, "We will talk later."

"Whatever," Aida said sharply. "Just be ready to explain yourself."

Both Aida and Cheikh waved goodbye to Bewaji before leaving. Noura watched her sister walk away, and she was shaky as she took her seat. It was as if she thought Aida would read her mind and see that she was thinking of kissing a woman.

"So ..." Bewaji placed her elbows on the table. "Is that the Aida that poured pap in your school shoes when you annoyed her?"

She smiled at the memory she had shared with Bewaji earlier during their walk. "Yes, she is."

***

Waking up first thing in the morning with someone's face on your mind and her name on your lips was a bad sign. Bewaji stared at the white ceiling, yet she saw Noura's round face, her pierced nose. She remembered the tranquil flow of their conversation and the silver jewellery Noura wore. She could even hear Noura's laughter, the way it sounded more like a cackle at times.

Hesitantly, she recalled the almost kiss. It was so surreal—she had not set out expecting that. Looking back at that moment, she knew she had wanted the kiss, but when she recalled Noura's nervousness around her sister, she was glad the kiss never happened.

Rolling over in bed, her blanket tangled around her, she looked at the digital alarm clock on the bedside table. It was a little past six in the morning. A meeting with Danjuma was slated for midday.

Later, he would take her to the location so she could begin her work.

After a quick shower, she slipped into a pair of jeans and a T-shirt before rushing downstairs to see that her father was still at home and Iya Gbenga had made breakfast.

"Good morning," she greeted her father.

"Bewaji," her father responded. "How are you?"

"I am fine." She noted breakfast was boiled yams and a vegetable sauce and knew she would be skipping it.

"How is your new job?" Fatoki asked.

"I think it is going to be a challenge," she replied truthfully. "I am going to the venue today. I have the measurements already, but it will be a different thing to see what I am to work with."

Sometimes when he looked at her, she thought he could see through her. It was like he knew every single thing about her, even secrets that she thought she had kept well buried. For reasons unknown to her, she felt guilt for not confiding in him.

"Can I borrow the Jeep today?" She needed to transport the paints to the venue, then she would see if she could work with a stepladder or if she needed to erect a scaffold.

"Of course, my dear." His attention was on the newspaper in front of him.

She drove to the restaurant where she had the first meeting with DJ and met him waiting for her outside. Together, they drove to the site of the proposed literary restaurant. The building had two stories, and within the high fence, the area was already landscaped. Inside, the place was clean. On the ground floor, there were boxes, some marked *fragile.*

"The forbidden forest should be upstairs." Danjuma led the way.

The room was a bare rectangle, but he had plans to place a divider in it. Bewaji would paint the mural on the eastern wall. She noted a window in the way of her mural that she would have to factor in.

"I will need that scaffold erected," she noted, looking up at where the wall met the ceiling.

"That can be arranged," he agreed.

Together, they discussed how the sketch would become a mural. Later, she started unloading her tools and setting up her space. As the day progressed, she felt her phone vibrate in the pocket of her jeans. Within her, she felt it was Noura. When she was finally free and able to check her phone, she saw, as she predicted, a message from Noura. The rest were missed calls from Ubeyi, probably wanting to know how yesterday went.

'Dinner tomorrow? My place, 7pm' Noura asked.

Despite her reservations, she agreed. Anything to spend more time with Noura. The only thing she would need to do to stop things from turning awkward was to ensure everything remained strictly platonic.

***

Sunday morning as Noura ate a breakfast of fried plantains and tomato stew, Aida showed up at her doorstep.

"Where is Cheikh?" She hugged her sister.

"Mum took him with her to asalatu," Aida replied then without further ado, she demanded, "How long are you going to keep dodging me?"

"I am not dodging you." She sat on the settee and reached for her plate of half-eaten food. The truth was she had no explanation for her behaviour. She said as much to her sister who sat down next to her, arms crossed.

Aida eyed her, but her aura was not hostile, only curious. "You were acting like I caught you stealing or something."

"I am sorry about that," she apologised sincerely.

"How is Taofiq then?"

It struck her then that she had not spoken to Taofiq in the past week outside one-word replies to his messages. She made an effort usually to talk with him on the phone everyday and to see him at least once every week in the name of being a good girlfriend.

Aida's question seemed loaded, but she replied with a curt, "He is fine, doing well."

"Is that so?" Aida lifted one brow. "It is funny. He called *Maman* last night."

The plantain felt soggy in her mouth all of a sudden.

"We all know she doesn't like him, so why did she give him her number?" Aida continued.

"*Maman* didn't want to answer it, so she asked me to pick up the call and invent some lie. I did just that, and Taofiq said he did not mind talking to me instead."

There was a tingling in her fingers and toes as she waited for her sister to finish the story.

"Imagine, he was asking me if anything was wrong with you," Aida narrated. "That you had been ignoring him for over a week. Naturally, I asked him, why on Earth would he be calling *Maman* for that reason. I asked him if you argued, and he said no."

Now she grimaced. Taofiq should have called her or spoken to her directly.

"Forget about him jare." She pouted. "I have just been busy. Why is he acting as if he is my husband?"

At this, Aida shrugged. "You are probably his wife already in his head. You people have been together since university."

She remained perplexed anytime she reminisced on the day she'd decided that she wanted to be with Taofiq, the suave charismatic student. She had gone for him despite rumours that he had a girlfriend at the time. Of course, he never mentioned this to her. Taofiq had been great company when she needed it. He was her boyfriend as an achievement, or a status quo, nothing more. Now here they were. He knew her family, and she was familiar with his. She felt nothing for him then, and she felt nothing for him now.

Already, her encounter with Bewaji was making her think outside boxes she did not realise she had placed herself in. When she considered it, the exhilaration she felt from spending half a day with Bewaji was nothing like she had ever felt from years with Taofiq.

"I am no one's wife." She wiped the last bit of stew with the last piece of plantain and ate it.

"I hear you." Aida finally unfolded her arms.

"Will you come shopping with me?" Noura asked.

"What is the occasion?"

"Dinner." She told the truth without thinking, then rushed to add, "Of course just for me, dinner for me and not for anyone else."

Aida shook her head. "I am not even going to ask."

Later that day, she and Aida went out to buy provisions. Noura wanted to cook something that Bewaji would enjoy. She would prepare dinner with the utmost care and attention, as a way to show her gratitude to her. She told herself it was to mark their friendship. She started preparing her ingredients for the coconut fried rice as soon as she returned home.

She left the pot to simmer and the grill on, broiling bits of chicken, by thirty minutes to the agreed time. She then showered, moisturised, and slipped into a plain dress. When the doorbell rang, her heart leapt. She rushed to open it and found Taofiq standing there, a box of chocolates in his hands. This would have put a smile on any other girlfriend's face, but her expression soured instantly. She was expecting someone else.

"Hey, baby," he said as he eyed her from the top of her head to her feet. "I don't like when we argue, I am sorry."

She accepted the box of chocolates from him but made no move to let him in.

"I need to apologise, too." She needed to make him leave before Bewaji arrived.

"You look good." He eyeballed her. Noura knew when he looked at her, he would see the short dress that showed off her legs and the plunging neckline that exposed her cleavage. "But I don't like this your hair. Why did you cut it?"

Her jaw clenched. Taofiq pulled her into a hug, and she relented. He was tall and had firm muscles from his daily workout routine. He wrapped her in a cocoon, yet she felt he was too hard for her. She found herself longing for softness, the press of breasts against hers. His hands snaked down her waist to cup her buttocks.

"Something smells good." His deep voice rumbled beside her ear.

"I made dinner," she replied flatly.

"It is like you knew I was coming." She could feel him smiling. "Let's go in, baby."

"No." She tried to extract herself from his embrace, but he held on. "I mean, the food isn't even done yet, and I am expecting my friends over. Let me go."

He dropped his arms and stood back.

"Your friends?" He frowned, marring his handsome features.

Looking up at his face, she suddenly wished she felt something more for him than she currently did. Why had that love charm failed so miserably?

"It's a girls' night out," she lied. "Gigi will be here, as well as some ladies from my new job."

That seemed to convince him. She let out a breath she did not know she had been holding when he bid her goodbye.

***

Standing before the red-brown door, Bewaji could not help but recall the last time she had been here. It was strange enough for her father to send her on an errand when he had his driver or his trainees to do that, but that persistent guilt had made her relent to his request. She had felt even worse when she'd gone over to Ubeyi's house and lost track of the time. She completely forgot about her errand until Fatoki called to ask if she had delivered the scarf to its rightful owner yet. Traffic on the way meant that she did not get to her destination on time. She'd considered turning back but had noticed that lights were on in the apartment.

Noura opened the door, all smiles, and drew her into a tight hug. Bewaji wrapped an arm around her waist. She could sink into Noura's pliant form.

"Welcome." Noura stood back.

"Thanks for having me over." She held out a plastic bag. "I am not sure what you cooked, but I brought rum."

66

Noura took the bag and motioned for her to come in. She tried to make her sit in the parlour and wait for the food, but Bewaji followed her into the kitchen. It was so tiny, she had to stand outside the door.

"See why I told you to wait there." Noura shook her head.

"What's for dinner?" She peered at the covered pot.

"Something delicious." Noura winked and handed her a plate.

Dinner was delightful, as promised. They sat next to each other on the carpeted floor, and she found herself telling Noura all about her current job. That Noura seemed so interested made it easy to describe how she had spent most of the day before setting up the stage for the mural and preparing the wall to be painted.

"I painted the base coat this morning," she chimed.

"That sounds amazing," Noura responded even if she did not seem entirely sure what a base coat was.

Bewaji nodded and scraped the last bits of rice off the plate. "This is absolutely sumptuous."

"I am glad you enjoyed it. I hope you're ready for the movie."

Actually, she had only come expecting dinner. Nonetheless, she was not ready to leave now that the food had been served. She helped Noura clear away the dishes.

"Do you mind horror movies?" Noura asked as she washed the used plates at the sink. "Because there is this movie I have wanted to watch for a long time, and I don't want to watch it alone."

"Is it that scary?" She tugged at a braid.

"According to what I've read online, it's the scariest film of the decade. Are you down?"

She assented. Back in the parlour, she settled on the L-shaped settee while Noura set the stage for their movie, switching off the lights and connecting her laptop to her flat screen TV with a cable. After starting the movie, she rushed to join her on the sofa.

As the first scene rolled, she huddled closer to her. The heat from her seared Bewaji's arm, which made her shift. Soon, they were drawn into the world of the film in which a group of women were trapped in a cave with flesh-eating monsters. Almost two hours later, the atmosphere in the room was as taut as the movie's unhappy ending.

"Well," Noura muttered. "That was extreme."

"That was scary." She officially had the chills. She never wanted to be caught in a tight place ever and was suddenly grateful that Noura had moved even closer to her as the movie progressed.

"I'll get the rum," Noura announced. "We need something to lighten the mood."

She switched on the lights on her way to the kitchen. Seconds later, she returned with the bottle and two glasses. Noura poured liberal amounts in each glass, handed one to Bewaji, then sighed with the first sip.

"I'll need to watch it again."

"No way!" Bewaji protested.

"There's a part two."

"You are on your own."

"Come on, it's not that bad." Noura reached out and rubbed Bewaji's bare shoulder. "And I know how to make you cope."

"How?" She eyed Noura over the rim of her glass.

"Music!" Noura's mood was back up. She rushed to her laptop, and soon, the first jazzy horns of a K. Frimpong hit filled the small room.

Almost immediately, Noura got on her feet and started dancing. She shuffled her feet to the music and spun her waist in time with the slow rhythm, transforming into one of Fally Ipupa's dancers. Then as suddenly as she had started, she stopped.

"What?" she demanded, hands on her hips. "Why are you staring at me like that?"

Bewaji cleared her throat. "You just need to stop showing off."

Noura sniggered as she swayed towards her, arms outstretched—she was Osun covered in honey dancing for Sango.

"Better join me." She clutched Bewaji's hands and pulled her up from the settee.

"I can't dance." She was already struggling to shuffle her feet.

"I won't take that." Noura moved closer, so close that Bewaji inhaled the scent of coconut, then she moved away like a nymph.

She covered her face with her hands, but it was true that with Noura's dancing, she had all but forgotten about the hungry flesh-eating humanoids that could see in the dark. Next, she felt Noura's hands on her waist, and the frisson coursed through her body startled her.

She dropped her hands from her face. Noura was trying to make her move with her. Noura lowered herself to the ground and came back up, delight etched everywhere on her expression.

Suddenly, her movements stilled, and Noura gazed into her eyes. There was a special kind of euphoria swirling in the depths of those brown eyes that pulled Bewaji's face down to brush her lips in a light kiss.

She instantly stiffened—this was not the plan at all. She made to pull back, and to her surprise, Noura stopped her. Silken hands cupped the back of her neck and held her in place. Noura glided her lips over Bewaji's own slowly. The first peck was timid, but with each contact, the women got bolder. She caught Bewaji's bottom lip between hers and sucked gently.

She could feel the heat radiating off Noura's body, the thunder of her heartbeat. She enveloped Noura in a tight hold, pulling her closer, waiting to melt into her. Her hand went to the small of Noura's back, where she caressed her and felt the woman shudder against her.

When she slipped her tongue into Noura's mouth, she tasted the spice of the rum and her sweetness. Their lips smacked as Noura pulled apart, heaving as though she had just run a marathon. A number of emotions flitted across her face. She recognised desire in Noura's half-lidded eyes, but there was also a slight frown on her face.

It was time to leave.

She let her hands drop from Noura's waist. "I should be headed home."

Without waiting for an answer, she bent to pick the car keys she had left on the centre table.

"Don't go." Noura's voice was low. "I mean, it's already so late."

Bewaji checked her watch—it was past midnight. She shut her eyes upon the realisation.

"Spend the night," Noura insisted, enfolding her in a hug from behind. "I won't do anything weird, I promise."

The truth was, she admitted, she did not want to leave. She had not wanted that kiss to end, and she was not exactly sure she did not want Noura to do anything weird to her. However, she saw that Noura was not exactly ready for this thing, whatever was happening between them.

"I'll stay," she acceded. "Let me call my dad."

When Fatoki did not answer, she guessed he was asleep. She sent him a message, then glanced at Noura, her belly clenched.

"I can sleep here." She settled on the sofa.

"No way," Noura declared. "If you're ready to sleep, let's go to my room."

***

Noura stared at herself in the bathroom mirror. She touched her lips then tapped them firmly with an open palm.

What have I done?

She saw her reflection but did not really see herself. There was a wild look in her eyes, and her lips were parted in the hope of more kisses. This was not her—this was not Noura Kanjuni.

She bit her bottom lip then stuck her tongue out. Groaning, she turned away from her image. She was not going to think about it; she just could not. She had left Bewaji in the room to have a quick shower before bed. She'd hoped the water would clear her head, but it had not helped matters at all. Rather, she replayed the kiss in her head over and over again.

She still felt the pressure of Bewaji's hands on her lower back; she heard her slight moan as she deepened their kiss. As she rubbed her usual bar of soap over her body, she found herself longing for Bewaji's presence with her in the small shower stall. Her body reacted rapidly to the mere thought of the other woman soaping her eager body. She could not help it.

Her shower took longer than usual. When she emerged from the bathroom, she found Bewaji curled on the side of the bed closest to the wall, fast asleep from the look of it.

Leaving the light in the bathroom on, she darted to the bed. She turned on the A/C and covered both her and Bewaji with the blanket. Noura lay on her side scoping Bewaji's back. She moved closer and closer still 'til she could hear the gentle sound of Bewaji breathing. Bewaji shifted in her sleep. Lying on her belly, she turned her face to Noura.

Noura waited for her to settle, then continued her observation. She peered at the peaceful features of her snoozing face. Her eyes traced the arch of her eyebrows, her small rounded nose, and her full lips.

Her hand would not stay still. Tentatively, her right hand moved forward to stroke Bewaji's forehead. She glided her thumb over her brow. The race of her pulse was at odds with the tranquillity watching Bewaji evoked in her.

Sleep came to claim her with her hand still on Bewaji's hair.

Chapter Five

As Noura rounded up the design meeting, her mind went straight to Bewaji. It seemed now that her thoughts spent almost equal time on work, family, and Bewaji.

A slight scowl touched her face when one of her team members came to ask her a question on the project on her way out the door. Now that the two-hour meeting was over, she only wanted to sit at her desk and take a break. She wanted to know what Bewaji was doing at that moment. Would she still be painting her latest project, or having a late lunch?

Settling down on her desk, she took her time checking her emails on the desktop before looking at her phone for any messages. Her chat group with her sisters was as usual brimming with messages. Now the main theme had passed from Rokhaya's honeymoon to Aida who was reconsidering getting together again with her ex, Cheikh's father.

She took her time responding, but it nagged at her that the person she wanted to talk to the most had not left messages for her. Bewaji had read the messages she had sent hours ago before her meeting started and had not yet replied.

Normally, this would not bother her at all. She usually thought the function that let people know when their messages were read on the other side was totally useless. Yet now, she obsessed over it.

She sulked then immediately chided herself. There was no reason to feel neglected because Bewaji was too busy to chat. She put her phone face down on her desk and made to look through the lab testing sessions.

She worried that Bewaji was keeping away from her after their kiss. She had not seen her since that night when she had carefully imprinted her sleeping face in her memory. The morning after, Bewaji had crept out before Noura's alarm woke her up. In their conversations afterwards, they had carefully avoided talking about the kiss, but it felt like an elephant in the room.

Her phone vibrated, and anticipation filled her as she flipped the device over. It was like fireworks went off when she saw a message from Bewaji. More notifications came in one after the other, and she impatiently waited for the photos to load. She gasped—there was an adorable selfie of Bewaji covered in paint. The colours not only stained her overalls, but also her face, with blue on her nose and green on her forehead. Bewaji made a face at the camera, crinkling her nose, a grimace on her lips.

Noura immediately forgot her earlier distress. Another photo showed a mural in progress. All she could make out was what seemed to be a forest.

'Caught up in paint' Bewaji wrote.

'*The paint suits you*' She smiled as she replied. Bewaji was gorgeous; she would look great caught up in anything.

It had only been a couple of days, but she wanted to see her again. The only issue was that she did not know how to frame the request. *When can I see you again?* No, that would be too forward. *I miss you?* Definitely not.

'*Are you free this evening?*' She sent the message before she could chicken out.

Bewaji took her time responding, and Noura almost shook in anticipation. When the message came, her keenness dampened.

'*I'll be working*'

Then another message came soon after. '*But you can come spend time with me? I'd like to see you again*'

She grinned. It was a Wednesday, and she usually did not socialise on workdays, but at that moment, she did not care. She noted down the address of the soon-to-be-opened restaurant and realised it was not too far from her office. It was on her way home from work if she took an alternate route, and she was not averse to this. She impatiently counted down the hours until it was five p.m. then she started shutting down, keeping her fingers crossed that her boss would not call up another impromptu meeting.

Downstairs, at the coffee shop owned by the company she worked for, she bought the black iced coffee Bewaji had enjoyed after their walk and took a bottle of water for herself. Thinking Bewaji might

be hungry working all day, she also bought
sandwiches and a pastry.

***

Bewaji asked the guard at the front gate to turn
on the generator as darkness fell. She regarded her
latest piece of art. While DJ had given her control
on his theme of the forbidden forest, she did not
want the mural to be too dark. Who would want to
eat in front of a disturbing painting? There would
be greenery, flora, and mythical creatures to bring
colour. The creatures from myth would not be the
headhunting gnomes from the tales her father had
told her as a child, but beautiful seductive women
from other worlds. It seemed she would never
outgrow her fascination with good-looking women.

The image of Noura danced into her
consciousness. She had jumped to conclusions about
her new friend. When she had woken up in Noura's
bed, she had been almost completely sure that
Noura would regret the kiss from the night before
and would try to blame it on her somehow.

It was not something far-fetched—she could
still remember how Ubeyi had filled her in on one of
her escapades over Thai food. That was before
Loreen. Ubeyi had become friends with a woman,
one thing led to another, and they ended up
between the sheets together. Immediately
afterwards, the friend had found God and wanted
Ubeyi to seek forgiveness for their sin with her.

Noura was full of surprises. When Bewaji
thought she would not want to see her ever again,
Noura pushed with frequent messages but stayed in

line by not blowing up her phone. Not only that, Noura seemed eager for the chance to see her. She struggled to control her delight—she was pretty sure Noura had a boyfriend at least.

She unbuttoned the top of her overalls and slipped her arms out, revealing the tank top she wore underneath. Her stomach grumbled in protest, reminding her that all she had eaten for lunch was boiled corn on the cob and coconut from the woman on the next street.

Her phone rang, and it was Noura outside. She rushed downstairs, just in time as the security guard opened the gate.

There was a huge smile on her face when the woman stepped out of the car wearing a skirt that stopped mid-thigh and a shirt that looked modest in the front but had a scandalously low back. Noura had changed her nose ring again, this one a silver disk that matched the rings on her slim fingers. There was a skip in her step as she approached Bewaji and threw her arms around her. Bewaji's fingers brushed Noura's bare back as she stepped away.

"I'm so glad you could make it," she said sincerely.

"I hope you're well," Noura replied, then laughed. "You still have paint on your face."

Bewaji swiped a hand over her face, knowing it would be ineffective. "Let's go up."

"Oh, hold on." She dashed back to her car and leaned in.

Bewaji allowed herself a brief glimpse at Noura's delectable legs and round bottom before turning her eyes away. She fanned herself with her hand. Noura emerged with two plastic bags.

"Is that what I think it is?" She reached out and took the bags from her.

"I brought coffee and food." Noura beamed.

"You did not have to." She pulled her in another hug. "Thanks."

From the way Noura hugged her and chatted about her day, it seemed the kiss had not unsettled her. Bewaji pressed her hand to her stomach as they headed upstairs. She had not realised how much she'd missed Noura until she saw her just then.

Upstairs had been transformed from the sparse space it originally was. Other than the scaffold, she had brought a folded chair, a cooler, and speakers for her music as well as an inflatable bed.

"What kind of music is this?" Noura asked as her eyes scanned the room and landed on the unfinished mural.

"Oh, that's from a compilation of contemporary kora players." She had forgotten that her music was still playing. "Do you want me to turn it off?"

"No, don't." Noura shook her head. "What did you call it?"

"Kora." She placed the bags on the floor next to the bed. "I have this thing for stringed instruments. Sit down."

"It sounds nice and relaxing." Noura moved closer to the mural. "But I'm not sure I can dance to this."

Bewaji tittered nervously. She joined Noura in front of what she had been working on all day. "Can you see the forbidden forest?"

"Is that what this is supposed to be?" she asked, but her tone was not antagonistic.

As usual, talk came effortlessly after Bewaji explained the idea behind her murals. She listened as Noura told her about the process involved in creating a website within a set deadline. They ate together, Bewaji choosing the tuna sandwich and washing it down with the iced coffee. With food in her stomach, she lay back on the bed and looked up at the ceiling.

"That looks more comfortable than this." Noura slipped off the chair she'd chosen and onto the small inflatable bed, her body stretched beside Bewaji's. "How come you have a bed here?"

"To rest my back when I need a break." She could hear Noura breathing. "So ... about that kiss."

She instantly felt Noura stiffen beside her.

"Yes," she mumbled.

"Why did you do it?" Bewaji shifted to her side so she could look at her face.

***

Several appropriate answers drifted through Noura's mind. *Because I wanted to know if your lips are as soft as they look. Because I have been thinking of kissing you since the bridge.*

"Because I wanted to." That's the one she chose.

"You were curious?" Bewaji focused on her.

Her eyes scanned Bewaji's open face trying to read for any signs there. Her question was not strange, but she was not interested in kissing any other woman that was not Bewaji—this she was sure of.

"I am only curious about you," she stated. "You don't hate me because of the kiss, do you?"

"No, I don't." Bewaji gave a small smile. "I was worried you'd hate me."

"No way," she blurted. "I thought you were angry with me."

"Why should I be angry with you?" Bewaji turned to lay on her back and stared at the ceiling. "I have kissed my fair share of beautiful women."

Did Bewaji just call me beautiful? Her brain picked strange bits to focus on. It took a while before it finally clicked what Bewaji was trying to say.

"What do you mean?" she demanded, wanting to know more about this angle of her.

"It means I would not dislike you based on a kiss," she explained. "You remember my friend Ubeyi? She was my first love, the first girl that kissed me in secondary school."

"I knew it!' she whispered.

"There was someone else in primary school, but I don't think I knew what love was then." Bewaji's laughter hid her relief. "You know, Ubeyi thought you were jealous of her."

"I was not." She immediately went on the defensive.

Bewaji hesitated before replying. "I fell out with my siblings after they found out that I am the way I am."

"I am so sorry." Noura kneaded Bewaji's shoulder.

"I am over it now."

The way she tilted into the hold of her palm, it seemed she enjoyed Noura's hand on her skin.

"Were you close to them?" Noura traced her hand along the curve of her neck.

"We had a weird relationship." She reached out and took Noura's hand, held it. "Noura," she said, looking into her eyes. "I don't think you are like me. We should keep this platonic."

Her heart felt like it was shrinking. She had hoped that the kiss would not disrupt their sprouting friendship almost as much as she had hoped for another one. She had never questioned her sexuality, and she was not about to. Whatever this thing was between her and Bewaji felt delectable, and she did not want to ask any questions but just to enjoy it. Oddly, when Bewaji confided this secret to her, she'd thought she had a chance to explore more with her. It pained her that Bewaji was not interested.

"What if I said I do not want to be just friends?" she asked.

"Do you?" Bewaji lifted her brows.

In the face of her earnest question, she lowered her lids. Deep down, she knew that was a Pandora's box she was not ready to open.

"Don't stress over it, Noura." Bewaji dropped her hand and sat up.

Already, her mind was spinning. She could not put in words what she wanted from Bewaji, but she had an idea that it involved kisses and much more. She followed Bewaji's movements and sat up.

"I won't," she said. "As long as I get to see you and hang out with you."

***

The weekend after Rokhaya returned from her honeymoon saw the need for quality time between the sisters. They had already convened at Khaira's house the day after Rokhaya landed at the airport, where the new bride had shared out souvenirs. Noura was content with a woven mat that now lay at the foot of her bed and a new set of lacquerware kitchen utensils.

All three sisters tried to meet for lunch or dinner outside once every month, an excuse to treat themselves, too. They had decided on an Indian restaurant this time. Noura arrived early with Aida in a tow, and they chose a table by a window as had become their preference any time they ate out. It was difficult to maintain a conversation with Aida when Noura's phone constantly vibrated. Bewaji was less busy, and she was thrilled at the rapid back and forth of their chat.

'How is lunch with your sisters?' Bewaji asked.

'We're waiting for Rokhaya' she wrote.

Despite her resolution with Bewaji, she could not forget the kiss they had shared. It came to her at strange moments, but as had become usual when she thought of Bewaji's lips on hers, she blushed. Her eyes flitted off the screen and found Aida's studying her. The ping from her phone demanded her attention.

'But you're with Aida, you should be talking to her'

'I should' she replied and let herself be honest. *'I like talking to you'*

Aida cleared her throat in an exaggerated manner.

"What's the matter?" Noura sighed.

"Nothing." Aida sipped her chapman from the straw. "I am just wondering when you became so attached to your phone."

She clicked her tongue. But before she could defend herself, Aida was up from her seat and waving. Rokhaya had arrived.

There were hugs and squeals around. After placing their orders, Aida and Noura grilled Rokhaya for details on her trip as if they had not been in daily contact thanks to their chat group. There was merriment around the table. Noura left her phone ignored and focused on Rokhaya's details on the dazzling stars in a night sky in a place with no light pollution, sunset cruises where Teslim and her enjoyed dinner on the Indian Ocean.

"Now that you've told us all this, I hope the lingerie served you well, too," Aida asked, wiggling her eyebrows suggestively. They had given Rokhaya lots of lingerie on her hen night.

Rokhaya looked away, a huge grin on her face. Then she deftly changed the topic. "Are we all set for this year's panorama?"

"Like we have a choice," Noura groaned.

"I am already sharpening my knives," Aida said.

Every year, their father held prayers for his deceased parents, their grandparents, who had passed away almost a decade ago. It was one of the three times in a year when the mansion's doors were open to a myriad of guests. Alhaji Kanjuni would call alfas to conduct prayers for the departed souls and afterwards came food and fuji music to celebrate their legacy. It was one of the few times when the entire extended family gathered under one roof. It also meant having to deal with the coterie of meddling relatives.

"I think we should all go together," Noura suggested.

"Rokhaya, can Hafiz pick us up?" Aida batted her lashes. They would all be heading in the same direction to the family home.

"Sure thing," Rokhaya replied as she looked over at Noura. "Will Taofiq be coming this year?"

Noura shrugged half-heartedly. Taofiq had been coming to the prayers for two years now. "I don't know."

"Is everything alright with you two?" Rokhaya asked.

"Yes," she answered easily, and noticed Aida peering at her again.

***

At Alhaji's mansion, the large parlour had been cleared, furniture pushed back against the walls, and plush prayer rugs spread on the floor. The sisters arrived late and crept in through the kitchen, which was not as busy as the outdoor kitchen where the hired cooks sweated over firewood. They slipped into the smaller room adjoining the larger parlour where all the women were gathered.

The room recognised them, and greetings were exchanged. Noura and her sisters went up to greet their Iya Tolani, knelt down to greet aunties, hugged younger step-siblings, and waved at cousins. Already, the drone of three men speed-reading the Quran filled the space.

As Noura settled on the carpet, her phone buzzed with a message from Bewaji. While she typed up a reply, she wondered how the women around her would react if they knew she had kissed a woman and enjoyed it. Without warning, a smile pulled up the corners of her lips.

Then she frowned in the next second. She had initiated the kiss only to see how it would feel. Besides, she and Bewaji were just friends now. Yet, she had not expected to like it so much, to crave more. Butterflies unleashed in her stomach when she recalled Bewaji's soft lips on hers, the taste of rum on her tongue.

She shifted in her seat, suddenly hot in the black abaya she wore, and loosened the fastening on the veil wrapped around her head. She was distracted when the flamboyant Aunt Yejide came into the room. There were muted greetings. She joined them while simultaneously trying her best to lay low. Luckily, Aunt Yejide went up to greet Iya Tolani.

"There goes aunt pepeye," Aida whispered in Noura's ear.

She snickered behind her hand—they always thought Aunt Yejide walked like a duck.

"*E ku ipalemo.*" Aunt Yejide's voice carried through the space.

Noura's brows knotted. That was a greeting usually said to families preparing to send a daughter to her marital home.

"Who is getting married?" She nudged Aida. It struck her how little effort she made to keep up with what was happening in her father's house.

Aida shrugged and tapped Rokhaya who was sitting beside her and also clueless.

"Your sister is getting married now," a distant cousin whose name and face Noura did not recognise quipped. "You mean you don't know."

She wanted the smirk wiped off this person's face, but Rokhaya was more diplomatic. "I am sure Tolani was waiting to inform us to our face."

Soon, the prayers were over. As everyone trooped out to the garden where food would be served, Aunty Yejide zoomed towards Noura. She knew what Aunt Yejide was going to say even before she started talking.

"Nouratu, how is your boyfriend now?" Aunt Yejide asked immediately after she had greeted her.

"He is fine." She searched for her sisters, hoping for a means of escape. They had both vanished with the crowd. She could never understand why this woman made it her personal issue to tell everyone to get married as soon as possible.

"What is 'he is fine'?" Aunt Yejide sneered. "When am I going to tie gele?"

She did not answer, but Aunt Yejide was not expecting an answer.

"Hurry and marry o, you see all your age mates are already in their husband's house," Aunt Yejide continued. "Don't be like your sister and have a baby without a home. Have you heard me?"

"Cheikh has a home," she stated.

"What are you saying?" Aunt Yejide frowned.

"I am saying my nephew has a loving home." She tried to keep her voice calm. "And that Aida has done nothing wrong."

Aunt Yejide's face soured. "Is it me you are talking to like that?"

Before the situation could devolve any further, she felt a tug on her arm. She beamed on seeing Aida, who briefly greeted Aunt Yejide then whisked her off.

"Do you know Taofiq is here?" Aida linked her arm through hers as they walked towards the garden.

"What?" Her voice raised. She had not spoken to Taofiq about the prayers, but he seemed to have invited himself.

"I thought I saw him talking to Daddy," Aida said as she rubbed Noura's arm. "Are you sure everything is okay between you two?"

She kissed her teeth. "Things are okay. You know I have never really liked him that much." Then she added as an afterthought, "I want to end things with him."

"*Maman* will be happy if that happens."

Rokhaya ran up to them. "Iya Tolani says we should help in serving food."

As daughters of the mansion, there was little choice. They walked to where the food was prepared and busied themselves taking plates to the guests. On her fourth trip, Noura carried two plates of amala and ewedu, one in each hand. She almost bumped into Taofiq.

"Hey, baby." He grinned. "I hope that is for me."

"It is for Daddy's friends," she said harshly. "What are you doing here?"

He did not take her tone or words seriously. "What? So there's nothing for your baby."

"Wait here." She rushed to deliver the food and returned to see him engaged in a deep conversation with Aunt Yejide. Noura clenched her jaw at the scene. Taofiq beamed under Aunty Yejide's attention, and Aunt Yejide bloomed under his charm.

"Don't worry mummy, it will be soon," she heard him say as she approached.

"What will be soon?" She walked up to them and crossed her arms.

"What else?" Aunt Yejide eyed her. "You are no longer a child. You better catch this fish before other girls do."

Taofiq laughed while her head spun. There was no way he would jump and finally ask her to marry him. What would she say? If he had popped the question just last month, she would most likely have said yes, but that was before she met Bewaji.

***

Noura opted to have Taofiq take her home. He'd had the temerity to bring his friends to her father's mansion so she could not even talk to him while they were in the car. Rather, she listened to them exchange details on the latest football match scores and tried to formulate a plan on how she would break up with him. They had been together for too long—she just knew he would kick back and that he would not make things easy.

"Should we stop to greet Mummy?" he asked once they had passed through the estate gate.

"Just take me home." She scowled. "And I need to talk to you."

He understood—he left his friends in his car and followed her inside. Closing the door behind her, she glanced at him. For the umpteenth time, she puzzled over her lack of affection for this handsome man.

"Is everything alright, baby?" He stood before her and crossed his arms. "You've been more distant lately."

"Yes." She dipped her chin. "I have been thinking ... about us."

Something flashed through his eyes. She thought it was concern. She cleared her throat and continued, "I don't know what you were discussing with Aunt Yejide, but we can—"

In the blink of an eye, he grabbed her in a heated embrace. His lips captured hers, and his tongue prodded its way into her mouth. His gentle touches were sensual and deliberate, yet she pushed him away. Caught by surprise, he glowered. In the blink of an eye, his usual relaxed mask came back on.

"My friends are waiting," he announced, already reaching for the exit. "Let's talk later."

The front door slammed behind him. Unconsciously, she wiped her lips with the back of her hand. His sudden kiss had confirmed what she now knew—there was only one person whose kisses she longed for.

She walked into her bedroom and threw herself on the bed. Taofiq was not a bad kisser, but what just happened had made her skin crawl. It was not this way before Bewaji. She opened her laptop and stared at the screen. She had done some searching online two days ago and found a number of resources that she did not have the time or will to read. But now, she felt she had to at least understand what was going on.

As she read through a funny article telling her not to freak out just because she is attracted to a woman, she found some relief. Yes, she was attracted to a woman, but that did not mean she had to start questioning everything about her sexuality. The article warned her that if the feelings she had for someone had become too strong to ignore, she should apply more thought to the situation.

Noura followed the advice to breathe and be calm, and to think. Closing her eyes, she thought back. Digging through the archives that were her memories, she unearthed something of significance. She had tried so much to forget about junior secondary school and Asnat.

There had been a competition involving several schools, and she had been completely entranced by the cute girl from a private school with short hair and pecan skin who had won the prize for the best speech.

At that time, all she knew was that she desperately wanted to be Asnat's friend. She recalled running up to congratulate her on winning the competition, the warm feeling in her belly when Asnat had smiled at her. The girls had exchanged letters when they went back to their respective boarding schools. There was a light bounce to her step when her name was called during assembly to pick up a letter. Asnat wrote frequently, using multi-coloured pens and always signed out with "love" and "kisses."

The euphoria drew to a complete halt when someone in her class called Noura a lele. She had not even known what a lele was, and it seemed no one wanted to tell her. Her classmates had preferred to snicker behind their hands and whisper harshly.

"*So Noura is a lele.*"

As soon as she found out what lele meant, she had firmly rejected the label. No way was she in love with another girl. Asnat was just a friend. Yet, the bullying had taken its toll. She had stopped replying to Asnat's letters and instead started capitulating to the love letters boys in the senior classes sent her. Being an early bloomer, there was no lack of male attention towards her. Now over a decade later, she recalled Asnat.

Could I have been in love with her?

Asnat's face had grown blurry with the years. Regardless, Noura could not forget the tenderness in her dark eyes when she regarded her. Had she been lying to herself all along? Was that the reason she found it difficult to love Taofiq or any of the numerous boys she had dated between secondary school and university?

Reaching for the pillow Bewaji had used that night she slept, she buried her face in it and inhaled. There was still the faint scent of peaches, and her body immediately felt aware. Her fingers ached with the need to touch Bewaji's skin once more.

Rising from the bed, she walked into the adjoining bathroom, stripped, and got under the shower. She thought the cold water would reduce her the flush under her skin, but as her hands stroked soap over her throat, thoughts of Bewaji on her mind, she grew even hotter. She glided her soapy hands over pebbled nipples, down the slope of her stomach, and massaged her inner thighs. She stopped her trembling hands before they reached the juncture of her thighs. She rinsed the suds off her body and walked into the bedroom on shaky feet.

Noura panted—she felt the imprint of Bewaji hands on her back as she climbed onto the bed and straddled the pillow and leaned forward, pressing into it. She wound her hips, ground against it; her tongue darted out to lick her lips. She increased the tempo, eyes closed in concentration as she saw Bewaji's face, felt her lips, her hands. Her chest heaved as she tried to picture Bewaji with her, Bewaji touching her and kissing her all over. The muscles in her thighs bunched, and she threw her head back and groaned Bewaji's name on her lips.

Later that night after the shuddering had subsided, Noura knew that there was no way she could just be friends with Bewaji. Not when she wanted her this badly.

CHAPTER SIX

On the agreed date, Noura drove to Fatoki's house. She met Bewaji in front of the house holding a nylon bag. The woman waved enthusiastically upon seeing her.

"Are you excited about today?" she asked as she got into the passenger's side of Noura's car.

"Extremely so." Noura smiled, and her belly warmed when Bewaji's eyes looked over her.

"I see you kept to the dress code."

She lifted an arm in flourish. "Shorts and tank tops on the beach is my aesthetic."

"Your aesthetic suits you."

"You look gorgeous, too." She took in the high-waisted shorts and midriff-baring lace top Bewaji wore.

Before they could start on their way to the bistro that Bewaji said had the best brunch menu, Fatoki appeared from the front door calling her name.

There was a slight frown on Bewaji's face as she hopped out of the car and met her father. Fatoki inclined his head towards Noura, seemingly unsurprised to see her in his house, and headed out with his daughter. She watched father and daughter exchange words for a few minutes before Bewaji rushed back.

"I don't know why he is acting like I didn't tell him I'm going out," she grumbled. "I think he just wanted to see who was taking me out."

"Really?" Noura laughed nervously.

"Don't let it bother you," Bewaji assured her.

The woman gave her instructions until they reached a nondescript black gate. Over a week had passed since she had met Bewaji after work, but they'd talked and messaged daily. The brunch was Bewaji's idea. Later on, there was a beach party organised by some of her friends. She had leapt up at the invitation, even after Bewaji had explained that it would not just be any ordinary beach party.

Inside, the bistro was well lit with natural light from the sun. She let Bewaji order for the both of them and took in the surroundings with her chin in upturned hands.

"How did you find this place?" Before Bewaji could answer, she offered, "Let me guess, Ubeyi, right?"

"Wrong." She crinkled her nose. "It's where I first met my current client."

Their knees brushed under the table, and at that small contact, Noura felt the beginnings of a fiery tempest in the G-string she wore. She budged in her seat.

"How are you sisters doing?"

"They are fine." She welcomed the neutral conversation and let her in on Aida's possible reunion with her ex.

"That may work," she reasoned. "Especially if they parted amicably."

"Their relationship ended because he won a scholarship to study in Japan," she explained. "As a PhD student, he could have taken Aida along, but she was not interested."

"I'm guessing he's back now?"

She nodded, then out of the blue, asked, "Will you consider getting back with an ex?"

"Well, in my case, it'd be impossible." Bewaji smiled wryly. "She got married."

"Oh," she gasped, wishing she had not asked in the first place.

"It's all right." Bewaji placed her elbows on the table. Absent-mindedly, her hand seemed to seek out Noura's. "We broke up a few years ago. She didn't even tell me she was getting married."

Noura gulped. She wanted to pay attention to what Bewaji was saying, but those fingers playing with the wide bracelet she wore on her left wrist clouded her mind.

"She did not want to tell me she was marrying a man because she knew it would break my heart," Bewaji carried on. "But she did not consider that my heart would be broken anyway."

"I'm so sorry," she said, hand on her heart.

Brunch was served shortly after. First came a pitcher of mimosa. She took a photo of the meal on her phone knowing she could not share it with anyone. Bewaji had become her secret, and as far as her sisters knew, she was spending the day at home. She was uncomfortable lying to them in this manner, and Aida in particular seemed to be very suspicious. She would have to make it up to them.

"Let's toast," Bewaji announced after filling two champagne flutes with the cocktail.

"What are we toasting to?" She picked the flute closest to her.

"To us. To new beginnings."

"So cliché." She giggled as they clinked glasses.

"How's the food?" Bewaji asked before she'd even taken the first bite.

Noura rolled her eyes and started on the eggs benedict. The chef had seasoned the poached eggs with chives and black pepper, and they tasted great. Closing her eyes, she moaned. She laughed when she opened her eyes to find Bewaji looking at her fixedly.

"It's delicious," she replied.

Bewaji took a generous swallow from her glass. "I am glad you like it."

As usual, the conversation flowed easily. It did not matter that they sent messages over the phone every day—there was still a lot to talk about when they came face to face.

"Are you completely comfortable with going to this party?" Bewaji asked for what must be the tenth time.

"I told you, I'm okay." She leaned back on the chair and lifted her face towards the open window and the sun.

"You don't mind that it's a party for queer women?" Bewaji pressed.

"I do not." She stressed each word. "As long as I am with you."

Bewaji tried to read her face then, it appeared, but then she filled their glasses again.

"We have another round coming up."

"What's next?" Noura leaned forward.

"This place does tapas, too. Then afterwards, you should see the garden."

***

The garden was a bustling verdant space at the back of the restaurant. They accessed it through a small wrought-iron gate. Bewaji held it open while Noura passed through it. They walked along a footpath marked with slabs of stones at intervals in the garden, with hardly any noise and bustle from the street.

The only sounds that reached Noura's ears were those of water from a pond nearby and birds chirping in the trees. She was a little unsteady on her feet thanks to the abundant flow of mimosa. She previously felt giddy with Bewaji by her side, but the cocktail had amplified that feeling.

Bewaji held her by her hand and led her to the pond where they peered at koi fish twirling in the water. Noura soon got bored with the fish, and she lifted her head and scrutinized the surrounding. The garden was empty around them, yet she sought a more private secluded corner.

She left Bewaji's side and made a beeline for an alcove beside a tree, knowing the other woman would follow her. Once she rounded the corner, she waited for her to arrive before reaching out and pulling her close. Bewaji instinctively held her, but she tried to step away.

"Noura, we can't," she protested.

She rested her hands on Bewaji's shoulders, kneading gently and wanting nothing more than to savour the feel of her skin.

"Please, Bewaji," she breathed. "Kiss me."

She stood on the tips of her toes and gently nipped at Bewaji's earlobe, tugging downwards. The fruity scent of her body wash titillated her even more when she lifted her head and saw Bewaji watching her with glossed-over eyes. Noura was unable to look away. Bewaji caught her hands and removed them from her shoulders.

There and then, she thought she had annoyed her by crossing the platonic line. She gasped in surprise when Bewaji pinned her hands up above her head and against the tree.

Her heart pounded as Bewaji lowered her face, then kissed her forehead, her eyelids, and her cheeks before softly caressing her lips. She strained, arched her back and opened her mouth to the gentle exploration. Her tongue eagerly sought hers in a slow, sensual tango.

She squirmed when Bewaji made her way to her neck, which she alternatively kissed, sucked, then bit into the plaint skin there. She could not help moaning—she wanted to wrap her legs around Bewaji's waist and grind.

When the woman let go of her hands, she immediately gripped her shoulders. A low whimper tore through her lips when Bewaji's hands started roaming under her top. Fingers glided up her belly and around her waist to fondle her bottom.

Bewaji brought her lips to Noura's again. They kissed as her hands moved up, capturing Noura's breasts in her hands. Her thumbs skidded over nipples that jutted outward against the lacy bra.

Noura shuddered under the blazing afternoon sun. She felt cool and hot at the same time ...

Loud highlife blared from her phone, slicing through the haze of lust and shattering the moment. Bewaji withdrew while she removed her phone from the purse, which she had flung to the ground earlier. With shaky hands, she answered the call and cursed when it turned out to be a cold call blaring with jingles.

Kissing her teeth, she rammed the phone back into the confines of her purse and glanced up to meet Bewaji's eyes.

"We should get going," Bewaji said.

Noura groaned inwardly. It looked like Bewaji was back to being hesitant. She wished she had put her phone on silent. On the way back to the car, she tried to ease the tension by telling jokes. Gradually, she was rewarded with Bewaji's smile.

***

Noura's body was on fire, and she fidgeted while driving to the beach. There was a storm brewing in her panties, and the only person to tame it was Bewaji.

"Can we not ditch the party?" She bit her bottom lip and looked sidelong at her companion.

Bewaji chuckled. "That would not have been wise."

"Is it because you want us to just be friends?" She moped now her eyes were on the road.

"It's because ... I like you, and I think we should take it slow."

She could not contain her chortle. "I like you, too, Bewaji."

"Besides," the woman went on. "It'll be hard to keep things platonic when you are all over me."

"I am not all over you." She clicked her tongue, but her objection was feeble.

She drove right to the lip of a small drop, then they both got out of her car. They gathered the drinks Bewaji had brought for the party before sliding down the drop. The water was a brilliant blue and the beach very quiet. Emkoria beach being slightly bareback, it was not hard to find where the group had gathered. There was music already, and a small crowd of what looked like around fifteen women of varied shapes and sizes all wearing shorts and tank tops. This time, Noura was not blindsided when she saw Ubeyi, who broke from the crowd and shrieked before running to hug Bewaji.

"I am so glad you could make it." Then she surprised Noura by pulling her into a hug, too. "Good to see you, too, Noura."

"How's Loreen?" Bewaji asked.

"She's here somewhere." Ubeyi smiled at Noura. "Come on"

She followed Ubeyi and found herself in the company of cheerful, friendly women. There were introductions, but she forgot most of the names seconds after. The only people that mattered were those Bewaji knew. The atmosphere was light and carefree, with merriment and drinks all around, and no one batted an eyelid when she held on to Bewaji's hand.

As night fell, the dancing got raunchier. The space they had marked out for themselves was dimly lit with rechargeable lamps, yet she could easily make out bodies gyrating. She preferred to dance on her own after Bewaji had gone to get some more drinks and small chops when she'd complained of hunger.

She moved to the music and felt another dancer brush against her. She stiffened instantly, thinking it was someone trying to grind up against her. She stopped dancing and spun with a few harsh words on the tip of her tongue.

A siren blared in her ears when she recognised the familiar form slow dancing with her female partner.

"Gigi?" The name left her lips before she could stop it.

Gigi turned at her name and immediately froze.

"Noura?" Gigi dropped her hands from around the neck of her dancing partner and jumped back as if the other woman was on fire.

"Baby, are you alright?" Noura heard the other woman ask, a possessive hand on Gigi's waist, but Gigi was only blinking rapidly.

It was like they had both caught each other with a hand in the cookie jar. They stood gawking at each other for what felt like hours before Gigi snapped out of it—she excused herself before grabbing Noura's arm and led her outside the circle of partygoers to a quieter corner close to the receding waters of the Atlantic Ocean.

Gigi began pacing on the sand. Noura followed her movements while worrying her hands and fighting the urge to flee.

"You're not going to tell anyone, are you?" were the first words Gigi said.

Noura felt affronted. "I won't."

"No," she added again for emphasis.

This stilled Gigi's feet.

"What are you doing here?" Gigi wrapped her arms around her middle. "In a million years, I never thought I would bump into you at a queer women's party."

I could say the same for you.

Was this not the same Gigi who had sat with them while they discussed marriage? Gigi who talked about her boyfriends, and had one as they spoke. Noura stopped herself there—it struck her that she had never actually met any of Gigi's boyfriends.

"My ... my friend brought me here," she explained, then she just had to ask. "What of Michael?"

"You just met her. Her name is Michaela." Gigi gave a sad smile.

She gasped. "You switched her gender?"

"It was the only way I knew I could talk about my relationship with you." Her friend regarded her with eyes that were overly bright in the moonlight.

"But you know me, Gigi." She reached out and touched her shoulder. "I am not one to judge or discriminate, Gigi. You really hid this part of you from me, and we've been friends for over a decade."

Gigi closed her eyes and exhaled.

"Noura, we are close, but one can never know." Then she took Noura's hand in both her own. "How are things with Taofiq?"

"Things are good." She gulped.

This could have been an opportunity to confide in Gigi, to finally tell another living soul her own feelings for Bewaji. Yet, she did not know how to talk about it. More so, she was not sure she was ready to. There was some relief when Gigi hugged her, from the implicit knowledge that they would keep tonight a secret.

Regardless, deep inside, she remained troubled. Today, she'd bumped into Gigi, and her friend was fine with her appearance in such an environment, but would other people be as tolerant?

Her imagination went into overdrive. What if someone had come up on them in the garden? She could not believe she had been so reckless. What would happen if it were Aida who'd walked in on her and Bewaji making out? What if it was, she shuddered, her mother? What if a group of thugs passed by and saw their beach party filled with women dancing inappropriately together?

"Are you okay?" Gigi asked, noticing her rocking unsteadily on her feet.

"I am," Noura assured her. "I just think I should start heading home."

She had knowingly walked into a dangerous situation, one that could end up destroying everything she held dear. With shaky hands, she found her phone and dialled Bewaji's number.

"Where are you?" Bewaji yelled over the latest Wizkid track.

"I need to go home," she said as she felt Gigi's comforting hand rubbing circles on her back.

Even through the loud music, Bewaji seemed to note the tremors in her voice. "Is everything alright?"

"Erm ..." She cleared her throat. "Yes, it is. I am just tired, and it's getting late."

"Fine, I'll get ready and—"

"No!" She panicked. "No, you don't have to leave with me. I know you are having fun."

There was a pause, then Bewaji's voice came low. "Fine, I will hitch a ride with Ubeyi. Goodnight."

Bewaji hung up. Gigi walked Noura back to her car and hugged her one last time while promising to keep their secret safe.

On the ride home, different thoughts assailed her mind. Her foot pressed on the accelerator, and she played her music loud. She saw her mother in tears and her father yelling at her, calling her a disgrace to the family. She saw her family excommunicating her, all because of who she now had feelings for. She had never felt this way for anyone. Up until the moment she'd bumped into Gigi, she had been elated and curious to see this feeling through.

When she reached the estate, she rushed into her home and her bed where she curled in the foetal position and tried to calm herself down. When that did not work, she rushed to the bathroom with the intent of pouring cold water over her head.

That was when she saw it on the window ledge, a dried-out bar of black soap. The hairs on the back of her neck rose. She had assumed that the so-called spiritual bath had not worked when she had seen Taofiq and nothing had changed in her feelings towards him.

But she had seen Bewaji first. It had never crossed her mind that a love charm would make her fall in love with a woman. The idea of traditional magic leading her into the arms of someone of the same gender was absurd. Yet, she had seen Bewaji initially.

She thought back to her reaction when she had first lain eyes on Bewaji. The attraction had hit her so hard, it had felt like her whole body had been thrown in fervour and she could not stand on her feet. That reaction could not be natural, she concluded.

The speculation had taken root, and she could not let it go. Her secondary school girl crush was nothing compared to these few weeks with Bewaji. She had never yearned for anyone as badly as she did for this woman. She craved her attention, to see her face, to touch her, to spend time with her. She felt nothing short of ecstasy in her presence; she lost track when she was with her—nothing else mattered. She felt safe and whole with Bewaji.

Already running away from her as she had done caused Noura's heart to clench painfully. In this short time, so much had been invested, but she could not be in love with another woman. She shook her head as if her feelings could be so easily dismissed.

She made a mental note to contact Fatoki early the next morning.

***

Like a thief in the night, Noura snuck in the house. This was her third time here, and the place was slowly growing familiar. She knew Bewaji would be occupied with work at that moment, even though she had snubbed her messages and calls since the beach party. This time, she had ensured she had an appointment beforehand. She arrived early and was led to Fatoki's study where she met him behind his computer, glasses perched on the bridge of his nose.

"Good afternoon, sir," she greeted.

"Noura," he greeted her with a smile on his face. "Good afternoon, how are you? Please have a seat."

She sat down and immediately started interlacing her fingers.

"How can I help you today?" Fatoki asked.

She had planned out what she was going to say in her mind, recited it over and over, yet she was presently tongue-tied. He waited patiently while she chose her words.

"The love charm," she began. "I used it, and I did not develop any feelings for the person I thought I would ..."

"Go on," he urged.

"It seems I have developed feelings for the wrong person." She cringed at the words she had chosen to describe Bewaji. "I want it to stop, this love charm."

Fatoki leaned forward and steepled his hands.

"Miss Noura, let me explain something to you." His eyes bore holes through her. "What I gave you cannot force you to fall in love with someone."

The world started collapsing around her.

"It alone cannot make you fall in love with a random person," he continued. "What I gave you only increases your chance at finding a soul mate."

"But," she stammered. "That is not what I asked for. I wanted to fall in love."

"And I have reason to believe that you have done just that." She glowered at him as he went on. "That you believe you fell in love with the wrong person is due to either you or society's perceptions. Love is a very powerful emotion that should not be manipulated lest there be dire consequences," he calmly enunciated. "What I do here is open the way, so to speak, for you to meet that special someone who has been written down in your destiny."

Noura's nostrils flared. Her nails bit into her palms as Fatoki persisted with his clarification.

He chose his words diplomatically. "You say you have fallen in love with the wrong person. I dare say you are not bound to them forever. Outside of advising you to prepare for heartache should you choose to let this love go, there is nothing I can do."

Her chest hurt. She was convinced that he had taken her for a ride.

"If I am to understand what you are saying," she hissed. "The bath, the incantation, all of that did nothing except increase my chance of attracting a potential soul mate."

"Indeed." He nodded.

"So they do not have the power to make me fall in love," she stated. "In other words, I only met someone, and fell in love with them on my own will?"

"Exactly that."

She groaned as she covered her face with both hands and drew in a shaky breath, once, two times, then dropped her hands down.

"Thank you for your explanation," she said before leaving the room on wobbly knees.

CHAPTER SEVEN

After yet another sleepless night, Noura gave up at two a.m. and switched on the lights. Her bed sheets were more rumpled than usual from her rolling around, running away from thoughts of Bewaji as well as from Fatoki's words.

She really thought that staying away from her would make these urges go away. Work helped in distracting her, and she had pushed through with the website and was set to have everything finished before the deadline. Spending time with her sisters and her mother also helped, but when she ended up alone as was inevitable, Bewaji's absence slammed into her. She missed the constant messages on her phone; she missed the late-night calls before bed, and she missed the photos Bewaji sent documenting the progress of her mural.

She longed for the laughter, for more kisses and caresses. She longed to hear Bewaji moan her name. It disturbed her that she might never again feel the incredible softness of her lips against hers. No one else could make goose bumps pop up the length of her arms the way they erupted when Bewaji placed a hand on her waist. She easily melted into hot lava recalling the way the woman kissed her neck, her cool breath in her ear as she sucked on her earlobe. Just below her ribcage, on the left side, was an unbearable hurt. She had not been able to sleep properly since she'd shoved Bewaji out of her life. Each night, she would lie in bed anxious with the lights off, tossing and turning. She could never shake the fact that an important chunk of her life was missing.

Is this what it feels like to be in love with a girl? she asked herself, then summarily erased that notion.

She lay curled on her side, her heart pounding erratically while she stared at Bewaji's number on her phone screen. The numbers danced before her eyes, taunting her to make the call. Instead, she looked through her instant messages. She had read through their conversation twenty times—from the very first hello she scrolled down through the daily *'how are you'* to the final messages that were all from Bewaji's side.

'Hi I have been trying to reach you, is everything alright?' Bewaji wrote five days ago.

'Are you avoiding me?' That came hours later.

'Did I do something wrong? Talk to me Noura, please' That came the next day.

She should not be thinking about Bewaji this much. It did not make sense that she missed her so deeply, unless she had already fallen in love with her.

She whacked that thought away with all her might. She wrestled within herself, and it affected her physically. Worse, her period had come along and made her even more moody. There were bags under her eyes, and her features seemed gaunter. Undoubtedly, people around her noticed. About a week had passed since the beach party, and not seeing or communicating with Bewaji had felt like being dragged through Hell.

In the early hours of that morning, she tried to watch a movie on her laptop and gave up when the light hurt her tired eyes. She climbed out of bed and stumbled into the bathroom. Staring at herself in the mirror, she looked like she had aged by about eight years.

"You can't keep on like this," she spoke to her reflection. "You just can't."

"But what will happen if you see her again? What if everyone finds out?"

She carried on the one-sided conversation, poking at the worry lines on her forehead.

She shook her head. "No one will find out. Look at Gigi. She has kept her love life a secret for years."

She splashed cold water on her face and marched back into the bedroom. Her target was her phone, and her hand shook before she pressed the dial icon. She had to call back twice before Taofiq picked.

"Noura, it's quarter-to-three in the morning!" His voice was gruff.

"Let's break up," she announced.

"Wait, what?" he stuttered, confused.

"I said I want to end this," she insisted. "I am not happy with you. Our relationship is a farce."

"Calm down, Noura." He was now alert. "Let us talk about this."

"I have made up my mind. You can't change it."

There was a pause when she thought he had hung up.

"You're having an affair, aren't you?" he growled. "You're throwing five years away for a bloody affair!"

She closed her eyes, her head pounding. "I am so sorry I wasted your time ..."

He inhaled deeply. "I am coming over to your place tomorrow. We need to talk this through."

"There is nothing to talk about," she yelled. "I do not want to see you or hear from you again. Don't make this difficult."

"Noura, I—"

She cut the call short and threw her phone on the bed, watching as it bounced onto the floor.

***

She could not talk to anyone about this before she had seriously considered the implications of letting her feelings for Bewaji grow unchecked. She was fine with it being her own little clandestine affair. Now she wanted to talk, there was no one to offer a leaning shoulder. Except Gigi, she realised.

It had been a huge shock to see Gigi at the beach party, but it was only in hindsight that she gathered she had not been exactly forthcoming herself. As the end of the day approached, she looked at her phone. After several days of her ignoring Bewaji's attempts at reaching her, now the calls and the messages had ceased. There was an ache in her chest, and she rubbed at it.

She dialled Gigi's number. When Gigi did not pick up the phone, she immediately presumed that her friend was ignoring her after their last encounter. Pursing her lips, she tried to shrug it off and turned her concentration back to work. Then her phone vibrated with a new message notification.

'*At a meeting. Can't talk now, what's up?*' Gigi wrote.

Noura flopped back in her chair and let out a breath before proposing, '*Dinner tonight?*'

'*I had a late lunch, let's do drinks*'

She headed to Gigi's chosen bar straight from the office. She was on her third glass of a sweet cocktail that had chocolate ice cream in it when Gigi entered the room. Noura jumped from her chair and waved.

"I was worried you wouldn't come," she said as she hugged the girl that had been her friend from childhood because their mothers were friends.

"I was held up at work. Sorry babes," Gigi replied.

They sat down and studied each other from opposite sides of the table.

"How is Michaela?" Noura asked.

Gigi looked away. "She is fine. I still can't believe you are not judging me."

"Come on, Gigi. Am I a judgemental person?" She lifted her brows.

"You aren't, but ... let me get a drink." Gigi signalled for a waiter.

"I was at the party as well, you know," she went on. "It'd be really hypocritical if I was judging you."

Gigi shrugged, a shadow of her usual vivacious self. "I just did not ever imagine I'd be found out like that."

"You're saying you would never have told me?" She pressed on with the questions. "Like forever and ever?"

"Honestly …" Gigi paused to address the waitress. "I'll have whatever she's having." Then she concentrated on Noura. "I never planned to."

"Why?" She found herself digging. "Did I ever strike you as homophobic?"

"Do you mind if I smoke, babes?" Gigi brought out a cigarette from her bag and lit it. "I don't pick those vibes from you, but you never know."

Noura wanted her to elaborate, and Gigi capitulated.

"I remember you joking about things in a non-committal way," she explained. "Remember when there was all that fuss over Aunt Martha's son being gay and you said you did not see what the big deal was?"

Noura racked her memory and found it. Mohammed had just graduated from secondary school when there was a huge fuss after he told his elder sister that he was in love with a boy from his class and his older elder had run to their parents.

"You never struck me as homophobic, Noura, but you weren't exactly pitching for the team, either." Gigi tapped her cigarette on the edge of the ashtray. "Then there was that time we went to Senegal and shared a room. One morning, I woke up to you looking out the window, probably watching the sunrise. At that instant, I thought to myself 'she's so beautiful' but I could not even praise you because when you noticed me staring, you became so uncomfortable. Even though I was not trying to sex you or anything, I mean you're my friend."

"Wow." Noura's laugh was nervous. She could not easily recall half of the things Gigi was narrating. Sure, she remembered sharing a room with Gigi in Saly. However, she did not recall the discomfort. "So how did I end up like this?"

"Like what?"

They had to hit pause as the waitress came with Gigi's drink.

"I think I am in love with Bewaji," she leaned across the table to whisper as soon as the waitress hurried away.

"The friend who took you to that party?" Gigi asked for clarification.

Noura nodded and sucked the last of her cocktail using the straw.

Gigi shook her head. "Noura, I don't want to ask you if you are sure, but—"

"I am so sure," she asserted. "I was attracted to her from the first time I saw her. The feeling grew once we started getting to know each other. Then I'd want to kiss her and hold her. I have tried keeping away from her. It has only been about a week, but I literally feel sick. I can't sleep at night, and I feel a constant pain in my chest."

Gigi took her time processing her revelation.

"Babes, you are so gone." Then she gave an unaffected smile that reached her eyes and softened her face. "It's brave of you to share this with me."

"I don't feel like a warrior." Noura slumped her shoulders.

"But at least now, I get to tell you all about Michaela!" Gigi announced, and true to her words, launched into the tale of how she met Michaela at a gathering much like the one at the beach.

"I am still amazed you kept this hidden for so long." Noura had done the numbers—Gigi had been with Michaela for at least a year and a half.

"If it's advice you want," Gigi said. "Keep it low, be discreet."

She jotted down mental notes. "Does your mum know about you, I mean ..."

"She doesn't." Gigi shook her head firmly. "There was one time I left my laptop open and Vicky happened to see that I was on a lesbian dating site."

"What did she say?"

"Babes, she just started crying, real tears o." Gigi scoffed, then imitated her older sister's voice. "'Please, don't tell me you are like that, Gigi, please.' I just said I wasn't, and the story ended there."

That night, Noura saw a facet of Gigi that her long-time friend had expertly covered up. Suddenly, things were not looking so bad after all. If Gigi had managed to keep her sexuality hidden from even her closest friends and family, Noura thought she could do the same.

When they went their separate ways home, she parted with a renewed sense of confidence.

***

The past week had seen Bewaji throw herself wholeheartedly into work. When she painted, she did not have to think about it, but the moment she stopped, she lost her self-control. The questions would resurface—what had gone wrong? Why was Noura ignoring her calls? She had gathered many answers, but the person she blamed foremost was herself.

After having spent most of her days painting at the restaurant, she was putting the finishing touches on the mural. She returned home on a Friday night after receiving a text from her father.

'My daughter, come and see me whenever you get home. Dad'

With Noura's abandonment came the need for alone time, and she had effectively dodged the few people close to her. At home, she headed to Fatoki's study and tapped her knuckle lightly against the wood.

"Yes," he called from the other side.

Squaring her shoulders, she pushed open the door and greeted him before moving farther into the room. The study was dark except for an island of light surrounding the desk where he sat engrossed in a book. He held a pen in his right hand that showed he was taking notes.

"It's like I haven't seen you in ages." He studied her over the rim of his glasses.

"I have been busy with work," she explained as she sat on one of the leather chairs opposite him.

"How is everything?" He placed the book he was reading spine up and dropped the pen. "Good?"

"Yes, sir." She peeked at the book but could not make out the title.

"Bewaji ..." He shifted. "You know you can talk to me. It is like we have not had a proper discussion since you returned from London."

She gazed up and into her father's eyes. "Can I really talk to you about anything?"

"Try me." He held her regard. "A parent can tell when their child is hiding something."

There was time she believed her father could read her mind. She was not entirely sure she had left that conviction behind with her childhood.

"In that case—" she wet her lips. "— I have something to tell you."

She shifted her gaze and looked at the mural she had painted behind her father's desk for strength.

"I am a woman who loves other women," she blurted. The quicker one removed the wax strip, the better. Without waiting for a reaction from Fatoki, she fired on. "Daddy, do you remember Temi? She used to stay over here a lot when I was seven or eight years old? We used to hide under my bed and kiss."

Her eyes darted to his face and found it blank and unreadable. The silence in the room would be harrowing, so she filled it with her words.

120

"It was the same thing with Ubeyi, my friend Titi," she said in a shrill voice. "I have been attracted to other girls since I can remember. And ... and Taiwo and Kehinde found out. We fought because they thought it was sinful. In the end, they kicked me out. They did not even care that I was broke with putting myself through art school."

She squirmed on the chair. "Now, I like someone who can't like me back the same way. Why should it be so hard for me to be who I am?"

The quiet she was trying to avoid finally settled in the study. She waited for her father to say something, anything, while inhaling shaky breaths.

"Thank you for sharing this with me," he said finally.

Her head shot up, and she gaped at her father. "You are not angry?"

"I have no reason to be." He leaned back in his chair. "I knew you would come to me at the right time."

She almost fell off the chair as all the wound-up tension left her body. "You are not going to ask about grandchildren?"

"I'd love to have grandchildren, but I surely cannot force you. If you want them, you'll have them."

She teared up. "Am I not unAfrican?"

"Actually ..." Fatoki moved forward, placing his elbows on the table. "This book I am reading argues that in certain West African traditions, the spirituality understands that some women are possessed with so-called male spirits and are thus attracted to members of the same sex."

"It is as though you have an answer for everything." She was rendered speechless.

He smiled at her, and she could not help smiling back.

"I can't believe this." She gave up. "Most parents would be furious."

"There are worse things," he reasoned. "You could be a murderer, a thief, or you could have abandoned me because I follow the traditions of our ancestors. I have an excellent daughter in you, Bewaji. I have no problem whatsoever with your sexuality."

She could have leapt over the table and hugged her father at that moment. Instead, she grinned at him from her chair.

"Thank you so much, Daddy."

"I have not done anything special." He laughed, then he asked, "How is Noura?"

"She's fine." She cleared her throat. "At least, I think so."

"Is she the one you like now?" he asked, his tone gentle.

She was not quite sure she was ready to talk to her father about her current feelings so soon. She evaded his question and rose to her feet.

"Let me leave you to read."

He did not raise any objections as she made to leave the room. She had a hand on the doorknob when her father cleared his throat.

"Remember," he said. "If you need advice from an elder, you can talk to me."

"Thank you." She looked over her shoulder. Fatoki dipped his head in response.

As she headed upstairs to her room, she could not shake the feeling that her father knew there was something deeper than friendship going on between her and Noura. Perhaps he could still read her mind.

***

"This ... this is wonderful, Bewaji." DJ stood akimbo, poring over the mural. "This is absolutely breath-taking. Your art has transformed this room. It even feels cooler."

His words lifted her spirits only a little bit. She had to force herself to smile. There was no logical reason Noura's continued silence should affect her this way.

Danjuma walked up to the western wall and studied it.

"You have mythical creatures and everything," he exclaimed. He examined the woman in the lake. "I hope that is not Mami Wata sha."

She had to snicker at that. "You wanted the forbidden forest, and all sorts of scary beings lurk there."

"There should be a sign up at the entrance upstairs that says—" he raised both hands for effect. "—Enter only if you dare."

"That or 'this room is not for the faint of heart,'" she suggested.

Now that the scaffolds had been taken down and overcoat applied, she looked at her work with a critical eye. The forest was composed of tall trees with shadowy barks. Above the canopy, she had painted colourful birds in flight while below, close to the earth, were little fairies partly hidden behind tree trunks. The fireflies flitting around the windows on the southern wall looked harmless enough, but she had based them on what her father had told her of vampires shedding their human skin and turning into orbs of fire. The greenery continued along to the adjoining western wall where a woman emerged head first from the inky waters of a lake. She frowned at the nose-ring she had painted on at the last minute.

"I am really impressed." DJ beamed.

"Thank you," she replied sincerely. This was the fruit of the energy Noura's absence had spurred in her. "About the other mural ..."

"I trust you completely now." He lifted his hands. "You can paint downstairs, paint outside sef."

"Does that mean I have free rein with the huntresses?"

At that, he gave a mock frown. "Let's go downstairs and discuss."

She let him lead the way at the bottom of the curved staircase where they met the security guard.

"There is someone to see you," the guard announced.

"Me?" DJ pointed to his chest with his right hand. "I am not expecting anybody."

"It's for madam," he explained, nodding in her direction.

DJ looked over his shoulder at Bewaji who shrugged. "I am not expecting anyone, either."

"It is that your friend that came before."

The air rushed out of her lungs. She wanted to scuttle back up the stairs and hide, anything to avoid confronting Noura.

"Tell her I am busy." She tried to keep her voice steady.

"Ah ahn. Bewaji, are you driving your friend away?" DJ lifted a brow.

"But we are working here," she said. "She didn't even tell me she was coming."

"Come on." He tilted his head.

She rolled her eyes. "Alright, I will be right back."

She pushed past him and out the front door, hands clenched into fists. As soon as she laid eyes on Noura, she paused in her tracks. Noura stood in front of her Honda, dressed in iro and buba in the oleku style, and worrying her hands in a gesture Bewaji now understood meant she was nervous.

"You shouldn't arrive here unannounced," she said by way of greeting. "I am at a meeting with my client."

Noura's eyes widened.

"I know, I am sorry." She looked down at her hands and added in a barely audible whisper, "I just wanted to see you."

There was a painful swelling in her chest. This close, she could clearly notice the swelling under Noura's weary eyes.

"Why?" She crossed her arms over her chest. She wanted to be angry at being dismissed and ignored for days on end, but with every passing second, her fury dampened.

"To apologise that I went M.I.A." Noura lifted her head.

Eyes heavy with meaning she did not want to start deciphering bored into hers. Her anger fizzled out. "We can't talk here. Can you hold on while I sort things out with Danjuma?"

Noura nodded eagerly. Bewaji stole one last look at her before hurrying back into the building and to DJ. As they looked through her sketch and discussed the specificities of the next mural, she wished time would speed up. When he finally approved the next piece, she could not return to Noura fast enough. The answers to the questions that had tortured her for days were finally at the tips of her fingers.

Noura was seated in the driver's seat with the car door open, waiting for her.

"Let's go for a walk." Bewaji looked down at her.

"Sure." Noura stood up.

"Why?" she asked when they were out the gate and several feet away from it. "Why did you disappear like that?"

As the words left her mouth, she wondered if she was taking this too personal. This was a woman she had met recently. Yes, they had shared a few kisses, but whatever was between them remained undefined. It should not have hurt her this much that Noura shut her out in such an abrupt manner.

"I was scared." Noura's honesty was a special kind of brutal. She stopped walking and turned to face Bewaji. "I am falling for you, and that scares the crap out of me."

Her face went slack.

"I thought I could forget about you if I cut you out," Noura gasped. "But I can't. It's been terrible. It drove me crazy, not talking to you or seeing you."

"So why are you here now?" she asked, brows pulled in.

"I don't want to run away any more." Noura reached for her hands. "I am so tired of fighting what I feel. I just want us to be like we were before. I really missed you."

Her feet moved forward of their own volition, and she pulled Noura into a tight hug.

"I missed you, too," she whispered in her ear. Then she stood back. "But Noura, please, don't ever shut me out like that again. I didn't even know what to think."

Noura peered solemnly into her eyes. "I promise I won't. I am sure of what I want, and I am not letting you go."

Bewaji's breath had temporarily bottled up in her chest. There on the road, under the scorching sun, she made a vow with Noura.

CHAPTER EIGHT

Noura drove up to her mother's house straight from work. She let herself in and announced that she had arrived as she crossed the threshold. Khaira's invitation to dinner was on the surface harmless, but she had been anticipating it. They must have noticed the change in her over the past two weeks, but now that she had patched things up with Bewaji, she was on her way up once more.

She found Khaira in the kitchen, tête-à-tête with Aida. They both looked up when she walked it.

"You're here." Aida stated the obvious as she grabbed her in a weak hug. "I was just on my way out."

"You won't be joining us for dinner?" Noura asked.

"No, I have a date." Aida winked. "It'll just be you and *Maman* tonight."

"Are you taking Cheikh with you on a date?" She frowned at her sister.

"Well, yes, because I am going on a date with his father." Aida rolled her eyes. "You would know this if you paid attention to our chat group."

Noura scratched behind her ear, and she rushed to greet her mother who was not her usual boisterous self. They definitely suspected something was going on.

After Aida and Cheikh had left, she settled down for a dinner of rice and beans with beef stew. If anyone could beat around the bush, it was Khaira. She kept small talk throughout, asking about work and paying rapt attention to Noura's details of the current sprint. Khaira dragged that conversation through the meal.

Afterwards, Noura washed the dishes. She was almost tempted to call it a night and leave when her mother invited her to watch an investigative documentary on a woman who gruesomely killed her husband.

"Noura, are you sure everything is alright?" Khaira inquired.

"Everything is fine, *Maman*," she replied as she scooted close and placed her head on her mother's shoulder. "I promise. It has been a rough few weeks, but things are getting better."

Khaira called her name again. "Noura, you know you can talk to me. I am your mother, and I love you."

She looked up at her mother's open unlined face, recalled the decade of no contact and how it had felt to finally be reunited with her biological mother.

"I broke up with Taofiq."

"Is that all?" Khaira prodded.

At that point, she started becoming exasperated and sat up. "What more do you want me to say?"

Khaira stared at her daughter.

"We have noticed that you have changed," she began. "We thought you would open up to us on your own, but you have kept quiet. You're holding something in, I can tell, Aida can tell, Rokhaya can tell. What is it?"

"It's nothing." Her mouth was dry. "Really, it is nothing."

She played back her conversation with Gigi and Gigi's advice.

Keep it low, be discreet.

Clearly, trying to ignore her feelings for Bewaji had affected her in a way that was obvious to the people that loved her. However, now that Bewaji was back in her life, she would know how to handle herself better. She would know how to keep things hidden from people that could read her like an open book.

"Okay," Khaira conceded. "Understand that we are only worried. If it's really nothing, then that's all right. Never forget that we love you, and we will always be here for you."

Even if I told you I think I am in love with another woman?

"I know," she said out loud. "I love you all, too. Everything is absolutely fine right now."

Khaira gave a small smile then cleared her throat. "We need to celebrate now that you have finally dumped that boy."

"Maybe later." She laughed. "Right now, I need sleep."

***

"There's brown rice, curry with chicken and vegetables like carrots, capsicum, and potatoes." Bewaji pointed at one plastic container, then the next. "I also made chapatti, in case you don't like the rice, and some banana cake with pistachios."

"All this for me." Noura placed her hand over her heart. "Thank you, my *chérie coco*."

She leaned forward and placed a light smack on Bewaji's lips. Work and other external factors had prevented them from meeting over an extended period. A few times during the week, she had driven down to the restaurant where Bewaji was painting her second mural during her lunch break. It was just an excuse to spend time with the woman she was falling deeper in love with.

They would eat together—however, those times were always rushed. It was hard for her to leave, and she got in trouble with her boss one too many times recently for resuming late after her lunch break. Regardless, it was always a joy to see Bewaji's face and steal a few kisses. At times, Bewaji would return the favour, appearing at her office where they would have lunch at the coffee shop.

"Are you now convinced that I can cook?" Bewaji quipped.

"I'll need to taste it first." She picked up a plate and started dishing out the food.

Tonight's dinner had been a long time coming. The idea was to relax indoors, and this time, it would be Bewaji bringing food. Earlier in the week, they'd talked about their favourite foods when the topic of cooking came up. Noura had teased Bewaji over not being able to cook until the woman had offered to make dinner.

She moaned at the first bite and found Bewaji looking at her. They both burst out laughing.

"You tried with this." She tried to keep her tone indifferent.

"That moan says something else." Bewaji smiled then tried to copy her moaning.

They ate over laughter and the sound of her music in the background. After dinner, Bewaji put Noura's feet up on her lap. Her long fingers pressed and kneaded until Noura fidgeted.

"How far with the mural?" she asked, basking in their closeness.

"About halfway through. There will be a grand opening next month. Will you be my plus one?"

She chortled. "Of course, even if you didn't ask me."

"What of the website?" Bewaji moved her hands up her bare legs.

"Done with that." She squirmed as Bewaji tickled behind her knees.

All of a sudden, a very familiar song started playing. A wide grin lit her face.

"Do you remember this song?"

Bewaji frowned and cocked her head. "I am not sure I do."

At that, she sat up. "Stop playing. This was the song when we first kissed."

"I was just kidding." Bewaji winked. "Of course I remember, with the way you were dancing."

"It's officially our song." She sprung to her feet. "Let's dance."

"I already told you I can't dance," Bewaji protested, but she wasn't listening. She turned and bent over, shaking her bottom against Bewaji's crotch. Bewaji grabbed her hips and burst out laughing.

When she was done playing, she held her real close in a languid dance. Bewaji traced her hands along the different curves of her body. She touched Noura's back, her waist, and squeezed her bottom.

Noura closed her eyes as her heart skipped a beat. There was a sinking feeling in her belly. Bewaji lifted her head then kissed her lips slowly. She traced Noura's lower lip with her tongue before deepening the kiss. Noura raised her hands and started to unbutton the tiny buttons of Bewaji's slinky top.

"Sit down," she whispered in her ear.

Bewaji allowed her to push her onto the settee and straddle her. That Noura was taking the lead seemed to turn her on.

She sucked on Bewaji's earlobe, kissed behind her ear then started to kiss her neck, dipped her head lower to place kisses on the valley between the swell of her breasts. She sucked and nibbled her way towards one breast and pulled down the balcony of the fancy bra Bewaji wore. When she took the nipple in her mouth, Bewaji moaned and slid Noura's dress up until it was bunched up around her waist.

Noura spread her legs wider in anticipation. She gasped as Bewaji pulled her up for another deep kiss. Holding the back of her neck, Bewaji devoured her mouth before she started kissing Noura's neck, returning the favour as her fingers found the dampness of her panties. She could not help crying out when Bewaji pushed aside the cotton of her underwear and stroked her stiff bud.

"Yes, baby," she whimpered and gripped Bewaji's shoulders snugly.

Abruptly, there was a loud pounding on the door.

"Open up, Noura. I know you are in there."

She almost jumped out of her skin as her heart tried to leap up her throat. She recognised that voice instantly. It was Taofiq. The pounding continued, so hard that she thought the door would break.

"Who's that?" Bewaji's hand recoiled.

"I think it's my ex." She looked towards the door where the banging had not ceased. Shaking, she got on her feet. "I'll go answer him."

Bewaji held her back by arm and shook her head. "You can't. He sounds mad."

"It'll be all right." She held her close. "Just call security while I talk to him."

She told Bewaji the number to dial on the intercom and hurried towards the front door.

"Taofiq," she called across the barrier. "I will only open this door once you calm down."

The pounding stopped as suddenly as it had started. She opened the door and immediately wished she had not. She thought she knew Taofiq, but never had she seen him so angry. He looked dishevelled, his shirt's sleeves rolled up and collar loosened. He regarded her with eyes that were cold and hard. Pushing past her, he headed straight for the living room. She darted after him.

"Wait, Taofiq, what are you doing?"

In the parlour, he stood transfixed, glaring at Bewaji who had her shirt off, a trail of red hickeys along her neck and cleavage.

"What the hell is this, Noura?" he yelled, pointing an accusing finger at Bewaji. "I mean, I knew you were cheating, but with—" his voice caught, "—with a woman?"

"Taofiq," she pleaded. "You need to calm down—"

"So what are you, a lesbian?" he spat, with emphasis on the last word.

"Please," Bewaji spoke up. "This is unnecessary."

"Shut up, you," he barked. "Don't interfere. This is between me and Noura."

He turned his steely eyes to her.

"This is absolutely disgusting, Noura," he sneered. "You broke up with me so suddenly, I had to find out why. I never expected this to be the reason."

She slowly inched towards Bewaji.

"I just couldn't believe it at first," he said more to himself. "I mean, even with the photos and everything, I just couldn't accept it ... but to come here and catch you red-handed ..."

Reaching Bewaji's side, Noura grasped her hand. She found strength there.

"I can't believe what I am seeing," he lamented. "You dumped me, *me*, Taofiq Olanrewaju, to be a lesbian?"

"What do you mean, photos?" She finally found her voice.

His lip curled. "I had my guy follow you. I needed to know why you broke up with me."

"What?" Her face turned ashen. Bewaji held her hand even tighter while her head somersaulted.

"Yes!" he hissed. "I know you have been running around to see your lesbian lover, touching and kissing her even in public, for God's sake."

"Show me the photos," she demanded shrilly. She stretched out a hand and was stunned when he slapped it away.

"Your father must hear about this," he swore. "Your entire family will know about this."

"Don't do this, Taofiq," she pleaded. "Let's talk."

"Yes, let's talk now ehn?" he yelled. "It's now you want to talk."

"What is going on here?" Finally, security had arrived.

Luckily, the security guard was Baba Sunday, a middle-aged man who knew Noura because she never failed to greet him on her way out of the estate when he was on duty. She also tipped him largely each year during Eid.

"Oga, this man came out of the blue and is threatening us," Bewaji explained.

"I am her husband!" Taofiq bellowed, slapping his chest. He shook a warning finger at Baba Sunday. "Stay out of our problem."

Noura was grateful to see someone who would be sympathetic towards her, and not surprisingly, Baba Sunday took her side.

"Bros, do you live here?" he asked gruffly. "Why are you shouting at night? Oya, make we dey go."

When Taofiq tried to resist, Baba Sunday grabbed him by the collar of his shirt.

"Do you know who I am?" Taofiq roared as he was led away. "Noura, this is not the end of the matter, I swear."

His threats only stopped once he was out of the house.

Noura sank to the floor, completely shaken. She sought solace in Bewaji who held her and stroked her back, whispering in her ear that everything was going to be all right even though she knew that her nightmares were about to come true.

***

Noura jumped when her phone rang. She reached for it and saw Taofiq's name and number flashing across the screen. A mixture of relief and fear thrummed through her body as she answered.

"I am downstairs." He sounded completely calm and normal.

"Taofiq, please," she started.

"Just meet me downstairs." He hung up.

With a shaky breath, she rose to her feet. She took an excuse from her supervisor and hurried down the stairs with shaky limbs.

By the time she had reached the coffee shop downstairs, he had already ordered something. When he saw her, he smiled and waved. She evaded his attempt at a hug and shot daggers at him, hands clenched at her sides. She focused on trying to centre herself, to draw strength from within to deal with this situation.

"This way," she said through clenched teeth. She did not want to start drama at work and would have preferred to take it outside, but he stopped her with a hand on her upper arm.

"No hug?" he asked.

She eyed his hand, then glared at his face. She shrugged his hand off and pushed through the glass doors. She waited for him under a flame tree on the other side of the road opposite her office.

"Taofiq, stop beating around the bush," she said when he finally approached her, a paper cup in hand. "We need to sort out this issue—"

"What issue? That you are now into girls?" He took a swig of his hot drink. "And you had the audacity to act all offended when I asked for a threesome last year."

"You said you had photos. Are they on your phone?" she demanded.

"You know …" He scratched his jaw. "I still can't believe that you dumped me for a girl. That's just wrong, Noura."

She stomped her left foot on the dusty earth.

"Are you going to keep on ignoring me?" Her voice raised, then she quickly lowered it. "You are the one who is disgusting! It is okay to have a threesome because that is what you wanted, but when you are not involved in the equation, it is all of a sudden immoral? You have no right to attempt shaming me," she spat. "Have you forgotten about Maureen? Or Fure, or any of your other girls, for that matter. Why are you making a big deal over this, Taofiq?"

"You are the one I want," he stated matter-of-factly. "You are and have always been the one I was going to marry. To be frank, you offer the most benefits, you're fine and classy enough to be seen on my arm, and Alhaji Kanjuni will be a great father-in-law."

Noura puffed out air from between her lips. Was Taofiq really saying he wanted her for her father's wealth?

"Besides—" he flicked at dirt under his nails. "My flings never bothered you, so why are you bringing them up now?"

"Taofiq, just give me your phone. Let's delete the photos and go our separate ways."

"I am not going to do that." His face was hard as concrete. "I have made my plans, and they involve you being my wife. Forget that girl ..."

"That is ridiculous, Taofiq," she protested.

"Noura, I don't think you understand." He moved closer until he was in her personal space.

She took a step back.

"Marry me. That is all I ask."

This had to be the most unromantic marriage proposal. She stood her ground. "I do not love you, Taofiq. I will not marry someone I do not love."

"Are you claiming to be in love with a woman?" he scoffed. "Rubbish! Let's be serious here."

He brought out his phone from the inner pocket of his suit jacket and scrolled through. When he held his phone up to her, she saw herself and Bewaji standing beside her car. Despite the darkness of the night, she thought she could make out her hand on the back of Bewaji's neck in an intimate hold. The next picture showed Bewaji and her, faces drawn together in what had to be a kiss.

At first, she could not place where the photos had been taken, but bit by bit, it dawned on her. This was outside Bewaji's workplace. She stared blankly at the phone screen. It had been an intimate moment, but in Taofiq's phone, it looked vulgar. She reached to snatch the phone but he was faster.

"If you do not want this photo to be forwarded to your father, Aunty Khaira, Aida, Rokhaya, Iya Tolani," he warned. "You will do what I say."

Noura was stunned to see the proof that Taofiq had really had her followed over the past couple of weeks. She blinked rapidly, fighting back the tears in her eyes. She would not shed them in front of him.

"I don't want to marry you." Her voice shook.

He frowned. "I'm giving you 'til five p.m. tomorrow to think this through."

He left her standing under the tree, quaking.

***

She locked herself in the bathroom. She had never felt so scared, so lost and bereft in her entire existence. Using her phone, she reached out to the one person she could lean on at that moment. Bewaji answered before the first ring.

"Hello, baby."

"Hi." She had held back the tears for too long. At her voice, the floodgates broke.

"Noura, what happened?" Bewaji asked, her voice full of worry.

Between gasps and sobs, she attempted to explain what had just happened, the way Taofiq had tried to shame her then later blackmail her.

"What should I do, Bewaji?" she wailed.

"Perhaps we can involve the police ..."

She laughed bitterly. "This is not London."

"I mean, Ubeyi's uncle is a high-ranking police man," she rushed to explain. "We can use him to scare Taofiq ..."

"What if I said yes?" She placed a hand on her temple, her head hurt. "Just to bide time until I get my hands on his phone."

She immediately dismissed the idea. Already, she couldn't stand the thought of seeing Taofiq's face let alone suffer his company. She feared that the next time she glanced at him, she would go into a fit of rage and try to claw out his eyes.

"Baby, he could have the photos in many different locations by now," Bewaji reasoned.

She sank down and sat on the toilet lid. "I don't know what to do."

She tore a length of tissue and blew her nose.

"This may seem like an impossible situation, but we will see it through. I am here and by your side."

"I know." She sniffed and wondered if that would be enough.

She did not have to say that she was not like Bewaji. She was not brave enough to stay true to herself in front of familial disapproval. Just imagining Aida and Rokhaya looking at her that way nipped at her heart.

"Do you want me to come over tonight?" Bewaji offered.

She declined. "I will sleep at my mum's place tonight."

Later, she let Gigi in on the situation. She had barely finished relating the story when Gigi started raining curses on Taofiq's head.

"That bastard will never succeed in his plans," she said vehemently over the phone. "If he tries it, babes, just deny everything. Abi does he have photos of you giving her head?"

Noura grimaced at her friend's blunt question but answered negatively. She and Bewaji had not reached that stage yet.

"It's okay," Gigi assured her. "If he tries to involve your father, just rebuff all his allegations, make up stories to explain the photos he has. Say, 'I was just playing with my friend now,' laugh it off. And when he is done being an asshole, let me know so I'll give some boys money to destroy his car and rough him up. Nonsense!"

She could not help snickering at Gigi's wild proposition. After she ended that call, she still felt that she needed more allies. Evoking the memory of the dinner she had with her mother, she remembered her parent's reassurances of love and support. Surely, Khaira would support her. She certainly hoped so.

***

"You look like shit," were the first words out of Ubeyi's lips when she opened the door. "Come in."

She hugged Bewaji. "Pele eh, we will sort this out."

Bewaji appreciated Ubeyi's assurances, but the situation felt like a lose-lose one. Confused and feeling stuck on what she could do to aid Noura in this unprecedented difficulty, she had asked her best friend for advice. Ubeyi had immediately asked her to come over, and Bewaji had been glad to dump her brushes. She could barely concentrate on painting anyway, not when Noura was in so much pain.

"What of Loreen? And Amara?"

Ubeyi waved her hand dismissively. "They are both fine. Let's deal with the situation on the ground."

They settled on the living room sofa.

"Tell me all about this," Ubeyi said. "From the beginning. Who is blackmailing your girl and why? How?"

Bewaji told her of Noura's situation. "He says he has photos, and that if she refuses to marry him, he will expose her to everyone."

"That's really messy." Ubeyi frowned. "It does seem like Noura will lose no matter what. Let me have a think. Do you want some juice?"

Bewaji shrugged. For her, the first option would be spiriting Noura away to somewhere that was safe from the judgemental prying eyes of society. Ubeyi rose from the couch and disappeared. When she reappeared, she had a pitcher filled with something green in one hand and two plastic cups in the other.

"Ugwu smoothie," she explained to Bewaji, who made a face but did not complain.

"You know ..." Ubeyi began pouring the blended juice into the first cup. "She could get married, and then do away with him, permanently."

"You mean like kill him?" She looked at Ubeyi from the corner of her eyes.

"Yes." Ubeyi filled the other cup.

"Seriously?" She raised an eyebrow.

"I am being very serious. This man wants her life. She should take his in return."

Bewaji stared at her friend as she would a two-headed stranger. In her mind's eye, she could foresee the aftermath of Noura killing Taofiq after marrying him. An intrepid journalist would likely unveil the truth, and the gossip sites would never let go of the headline, "Woman kills husband to elope with lesbian lover."

"Who gets away with murder these days?" She kissed her teeth. She could already picture the vitriolic comments online. "I came here for something practical."

"See—" Ubeyi sat down close beside her. "That guy could spend the rest of his life blackmailing her. If he has those photos, he will forever dangle it over her head, and she will forever be dancing to his tune."

Bewaji pounded a fist against the leather sofa, helpless.

***

Noura moved through the motions as if they had been programmed into her. She sat at a meeting when she should have been on her way out of the office, then sat through traffic. By the time she reached her mother's house, it was ten p.m.

Wryly noticing that she now had less than twenty-four hours to before Taofiq's ultimatum ran out, she skipped dinner and had a shower before attempting to sleep in the spare bedroom. When sleep proved unfruitful, she slipped into Aida's room and lay on the bed with Cheikh between them.

She watched them under the colourful night-lights that Cheikh needed to sleep. How would they react when shit hit the fan? She looked at her nephew's peaceful resting face and leaned forward to sniff his baby lotion scent.

She turned her gaze to her beautiful sister, eyebrows drawn together in her sleep. Would Aida remain her number one supporter, as she had always been? Or would she also find her own sister disgusting? Tears burned behind her eyelids as she imagined Aida trying to keep Cheikh away from her, afraid of her somehow infecting him.

It scared her, but she had made up her mind. She would have to tell her mother and seek her advice. She waited until it was five a.m., knowing that Khaira would be awake for the early morning prayers. She caught her mum coming out of the bathroom after doing her ablutions.

"Noura, what is happening?" Khaira's gaze was pained. "Talk to me."

She sat on the bed beside her daughter, her prayers momentarily postponed.

"*Maman*," she sighed. "I am ready to talk. Will you promise to listen?"

"Of course." Khaira nodded and seized Noura's hands.

Noura clasped her mother's soft hands, then she started talking. She told her mother that she had met someone and had fallen in love with that person, not mentioning the person's sex. She informed Khaira of the break up and how now Taofiq did not want to let her go and was trying to blackmail her with incriminating photos of her and her new lover.

"Is that what has been disturbing you?" Khaira did not look bothered. "Noura, this is nothing. You know I never liked Taofiq. I am happy you have found someone new, and I am sure he will be better for you than that boy. I will talk to Taofiq about those threats of his."

"I did not say he." Her voice was low.

"Sorry?" Khaira squinted.

"I never said that my new love is a he," she repeated.

146

"What does that mean?" Khaira murmured.

She inhaled. "It means I am in love with a woman."

After she rushed out the words, she dared to look at her mother. A thousand emotions flickered across Khaira's face before she let go of Noura's hands as though they were made of bare electric current.

Noura choked at the abandonment.

"No ..." Khaira shook her head, stuttering. "No ... that ... no."

The world shattered around her. It was exactly what she had feared. She ran out of Khaira's room and the house in her pyjamas and bare feet, tears streaking down her face.

CHAPTER NINE

She was going to take a half-day from work. In fact, she felt like she needed a chunk off her leave days. Unfortunately, she had only just started working at her new job and was on six months' probation.

Noura had barely got into the office and settled down in her chair when her highlife ringtone sounded. She was beginning to dislike the song. A sense of impending doom hit her when she saw Uncle Bola's name on the screen. She held her phone, debating whether to answer. At the last minute, she pressed the accept button.

"Good morning, Uncle," she greeted.

"Noura, how are you?" His voice did not broker any alarm, but she just knew. The last time Uncle Bola had called her, it had been when her parents had sent him to dissuade her from moving out of the family home.

"I am fine, sir," she replied, heart performing breakdance moves in her chest.

"That's good," he replied, then paused before continuing. "Noura, your father just gave me some disturbing news that I know cannot be true."

She rubbed at her forehead while her father's younger brother spoke.

"If you and Taofiq are fighting, it is no problem, we will intervene," he continued. "I don't even know why Taofiq will suggest such an abominable thing. I am sure your father will warn him dearly. Are you listening?"

She took her time answering. "Yes, sir."

"Good. You should come to the house after work today. Let us clear the air surrounding these accusations. Don't worry, we know it is not true."

By the time Uncle Bola hung up, she was feeling nihilistic. She did not want to care anymore. Let everyone abandon her like she had acquired some infectious disease when the only crime she'd committed was falling in love with Bewaji.

As if summoned by her thought, Bewaji's call came through. She only felt slightly relieved when she heard the mellow voice.

"I have been trying to reach you," Bewaji stated.

"I couldn't talk then." Her voice was shaky. She had ignored all calls after the failure of her confiding in her mother. She got up abruptly from her chair and rushed to the toilets.

"How are you? Has Taofiq contacted you since?"

"I think he has already told my father." She locked the door behind her.

A stream of expletives emerged from the other side of the phone.

"I told my mother," she revealed.

"How did she take it?"

"How do you think?" she snapped. She did not mean to, so she hastily apologised. That wound was still so raw.

"It's alright, baby," Bewaji cajoled. "I know it must be hard for you."

She drew in a shaky breath as she narrated the events of the early morning. "I can't stand this ... My own mother looked at me as if I was a stranger."

"I am so sorry."

Bewaji sounded feeble, but she kept on heaping on the bad news.

"And now, I am being summoned to the mansion." She shut her eyes tight in an effort to control the tears. "Do you know how stupidly traditional my family is? I don't know what to do."

"Listen, Noura," Bewaji tried to reassure her. "Even if your family is against you, I am here for you, and I will support you."

She thanked her, even though she felt they were completely powerless in the face of the current situation.

"How did you do it?" she asked. "How was it when your siblings kicked you out?"

"It was hard," Bewaji confessed. "I don't think I can ever get over it, but I have to continue moving forward ... also, I am lucky that my dad supports me."

"Fatoki!" she exclaimed. "He is okay with you dating women?"

She was surprised when Bewaji replied affirmatively. A reluctant smile touched her face as Bewaji told her how she came out to her father in his study one night.

Noura fervently wished for such support from her family, yet she could not help but feel pessimistic.

***

On the way to her father's house, she recalled an event that had made a lasting impact on her and Aida. When she was eleven years old and Aida twelve, an aunt—one of her father's younger cousins who was living in them while doing an internship—became pregnant.

Alhaji Kanjuni had called all the young girls in the house at that time to the living room where they had witnessed Aunty Mulika's humiliation. Before he began berating Aunty Mulika, he had explained that he did not want any of the young girls living under his roof to follow in her disgraceful lead. Rokhaya was considered too young to be there, but Noura had stood slightly behind Aida at the time.

Their father had rebuked Aunty Mulika, made her kneel down while she was forced to detail her long list of sins from falling in love with a boy from the wrong tribe to allowing him to impregnate her. Aunty Mulika had shuddered uncontrollably, her head bowed under the burden of several pairs of judgemental eyes.

It should have been ingrained in Noura then that to avoid a similar ordeal, one should stick to

Alhaji Kanjuni's moral code. However, she and Aida had hated the whole thing in varying degrees, Aida to the point of following Aunty Mulika's example—she lived her life the way she wanted to and damn the consequences.

Noura, on the other hand, had always been more malleable. See how easily she had accepted the summons, for one. Aida would never have agreed to show up. She tried to imagine who would have the front seat to the theatre of her own humiliation. Already, she knew to follow Gigi's advice in order to avoid worsening the situation, she would refute any of Taofiq's claims. The fact that she had been called over meant that she had a chance to explain herself. Surely, if Taofiq had shown anyone the photos, she would have been disowned immediately, she reasoned.

The house was quieter than usually when she entered. She was directed to the parlour upstairs, and in there, saw her father, her stepmother, and Taofiq. Alhaji Kanjuni sat on his throne, a heavy, gold-gilded chair while his wife sat beside him in a chair that was smaller but no less elaborate. Taofiq was on the white leather sofa to the left of her father, leaning forward as though whispering his poison into Alhaji Kanjuni's ear.

She greeted the elders and ignored him.

"Noura, you won't greet Taofiq?" That was Iya Tolani.

"No," she spat.

"Baby, come on—" Taofiq said while she shot daggers at him.

"Don't you dare ..." She pointed a finger at him in warning.

"I did not call you here to fight." Alhaji Kanjuni shifted on his chair, and his wife with him. "I just want to clear the air."

She was not offered a seat, but even if she was, she was sure she would not accept it. She preferred to stand and face whatever was coming head on. She could hear her own rage breathing in her ears as her father continued.

"Taofiq here— he motioned towards where Taofiq sat with his left hand, "—is saying that you ended things with him. That in itself is nothing spectacular. However, he is giving unbelievable reasons as to why. I almost slapped him, but he claims to have evidence."

"Daddy," Noura said, her voice steady and low-pitched. "I have just seen Taofiq's true colours. He is a manipulative liar. I broke up with him, yes, and he should have taken it in stride. Instead, he is here running about like a headless chicken, spreading slander."

She did not know what Taofiq had discussed with her father before her arrival, but she sensed that she had to get her piece out there as soon as possible.

"Whatever Taofiq has told you—" she swallowed, "—is untrue. The fact is I do not love him, I never did. I ask that as my father, you make him leave me alone and put a stop to his blackmailing me."

Alhaji Kanjuni cleared his throat. "Taofiq has made some very serious allegations."

"His allegations are untrue," she insisted.

"Untrue?" Taofiq flared, jumping to his feet. "Noura, we both know who is lying here. Don't make me expose you."

Inside, she trembled, but outside, she maintained her composure.

"What do you have on me, Taofiq?" She locked eyes with him. "Photos of me and my friend? Your images do not prove anything about me."

Catching the flash of unease in his eyes at her words, she fired on. "Go on, bring your proof and show it, then. Show all of us."

Taofiq thought he knew her. It was true that for most of her life, she had consistently bent under the will of her father, but for years, she had begun pushing back. At that moment, she was sure that he had no real intention of showing the photos to her parents. He genuinely thought that the threat of exposure was enough to make her agree to his unreasonable demands.

"Fine."

On the surface, he seemed sure of himself, but she could pick the slight tremors in his voice. Whipping out his phone from the pocket of his jeans, he approached Alhaji Kanjuni.

Noura's heart blocked in her throat as Taofiq showed her father his proof. It was a wild guess, but she did not think he had any photos that would invariably reveal the truth of her relationship with Bewaji. Nevertheless, the uncertainty remained below her stomach. From what he had shown her the day before, she found room to wiggle around, but what if he had more risqué shots?

"See what your daughter is doing?" Taofiq said.

Alhaji Kanjuni took the phone from Taofiq's hands and held it out to her. "Noura, what is this?"

She took the phone—it dropped out of her hands. She bent to pick it up from the floor and looked at photos of her and Bewaji. Taofiq must have had her followed from the time she broke up with him.

The earliest images were of when she met Bewaji to apologise to her after cutting her off. It showed her holding Bewaji's hands and staring earnestly into her eyes in a moment that had been so important for her.

She saw photo after photo. Baring that time in the garden, she and Bewaji had only ever been intimate behind closed doors or under the cover of darkness. Whoever Taofiq had hired took photos of them kissing in front of her car, but that was a dark night when the streetlights had been off due to a power cut. All that could be made out were two heads meeting. For all, she could have been whispering into a friend's ear.

There were photos of Bewaji holding her hand as they walked to buy boiled corn from the woman who had set up shop close to the restaurant. Noura recalled the heat of that afternoon—they had paused, and Bewaji had stroked her cropped hair. Whoever Taofiq had sent to follow them had also captured a photo of them at that moment.

She almost laughed as she scrolled through. Was this the evidence Taofiq was so sure of? All this could easily be explained as two friends just hanging out.

"Daddy, this is me and my close friend Bewaji." She looked up and into her father's eyes. "I don't know what Taofiq has told you about me, but this only shows two friends together. I see nothing untoward here. What did you see when you looked at these photos?"

Alhaji Kanjuni coughed lightly and avoided her gaze.

"Let me see the photos, Noura." Iya Tolani stretched a hand.

She handed the phone to her stepmother who actually laughed as she examined them.

"Taofiq," she said. "You don't know that girls can be close in this manner."

"Iya Tolani." Taofiq's hands flew in the air as he rushed to explain. "I know what I am saying. That girl is Noura's lover. I know Noura is involved with her. I caught the girl half-naked in Noura's house."

"Can you see how confused Taofiq is?" Noura clicked her tongue. "Daddy, you need to call him to order."

"I know what I am saying." Taofiq raised his voice. "Noura, we both know you are nothing but a filthy lesbian."

He moved so quickly, she was caught by surprise. He grasped her upper arm roughly. His nostrils flared as he shook her, demanding that she tell the truth to her parents.

"That is enough, Taofiq." Alhaji Kanjuni's voice was stern and cut through Taofiq's fury.

Noura pulled away immediately and found herself drawn into Iya Tolani's embrace.

"First of all, Taofiq ..." Her father's voice brokered no argument. "Delete those images from your phone."

This was the part of her father that his business rivals feared. His eyes were cold as steel and his voice dangerously low, each word he said pregnant with the veiled threats. Taofiq did as was ordered with shaky hands.

"How is Mr. Abdul doing these days? You are still working for him, aren't you, Taofiq?" he asked leisurely.

"Yes, sir."

"I am sure you understand that you can lose your job like this." Alhaji Kanjuni clicked his fingers. It was a pleasure seeing Taofiq shake in his shoes. "Now get out of my sight."

Taofiq rushed out of the room, taking all of Noura's worry and fear with him. She sagged against her stepmother's arms.

"Stupid boy," Alhaji Kanjuni uttered after Taofiq had rushed out. "I knew no daughter of mine would ever be affected by the spirit of homosexuality."

"It is unheard of in your family line," Iya Tolani said, her voice sharp in Noura's ear.

As Noura listened to her father and stepmother denounce the spirit of homosexuality, she did not exactly feel relief. The situation with Taofiq seemed to have been solved, but that was just for now. She considered the continued pressure to marry, and this came interspersed with thoughts of Bewaji.

In her mind's eye, she saw Bewaji's smile. She felt the sense of peace and belonging that always covered her when in her presence. She saw the smiles, and she heard the laughter that came with being with her.

Yes, she could continue seeing her on the low, but would Taofiq give up so easily? And if he did, how many other Taofiqs would there be in the future? People who would attempt to turn this beautiful thing she shared with Bewaji into something revolting? People who may have stronger evidence than photos of them hugging or holding hands? Such people would always use her family to threaten her into submission.

"There is no one who practices such evils in my family." Alhaji Kanjuni affirmed his wife's words.

"What if there is?" The words had escaped Noura's lips. There was no backing down now.

"Excuse me?" Her father grimaced.

She drew in a shaky breath. "What if I am in love with another woman?"

Iya Tolani immediately flung her out of her hold.

"Olorun ma je!" She clicked the fingers of both hands over her head.

"Mummy—" she glanced from her stepmother's alarmed face to her father's disapproving one, and her heartbeat accelerated even more. "Daddy, what I am trying to say is I am in love with a woman."

Alhaji Kanjuni's eyes tripled in size, and Iya Tolani's jaw went slack, but Noura pushed on.

"And I am okay with this. I do not believe what I feel is a sin. I do not believe any kind of love is wrong."

"Will you shut up!" Her father jumped from his throne-like chair as if someone had placed a nail under his bottom. "Stupid girl! There must be something wrong with you, to make you speak such abominations before me."

Noura hated this situation so much, but she felt she had no choice other than facing it through. She had always been open with her family, her sisters, even her distant father—she knew she could not live a lie. Her family had always been the forefront, the beginning, the end, the all and everything in-between. Now all she wanted was their acceptance, and even that seemed so impossible.

Her father's hands trembled as he clenched them to his side. Iya Tolani ran up to him, clung to his thick shoulders.

Noura watched her stepmother calm her father down in appeasing tones. "Please do not despair, this case is not closed."

"What are you saying?" her father barked, but his eyes were on Noura.

"I am saying that Noura does not know what she is saying. She is still a child," Iya Tolani cajoled. "And if she is truly affected by that spirit, God forbid, she can be cured. There are men of spiritual might who can cure Noura of this spirit of lesbianism discreetly, and no one will have to know."

Right there and then, she wanted the ground to open up and claim her. She knew her father would be disapproving, but this was not expected. She wrapped her arms around her middle. She had heard of what so-called healers did to cure victims they believed were under the influence of malevolent spirits.

"My daughter will not go anywhere!"

Those words were rays of light dispersing her despair.

Spinning around, she saw her mother looking atypically disturbed. The flowing gown she wore was rumpled and falling over one shoulder, and her head tie looked as if it had been hastily thrown on her head. Khaira's slippers smacked the marble floor as she marched into the room.

"Noura will not be sent anywhere!" Khaira shrieked.

New hope flared in her heart as her mother stood by her.

The shock of Khaira's arrival had left both her father and stepmother flabbergasted. However, they soon jolted into action.

"The daughter of a wayward woman, no wonder." Iya Tolani conjured up the bitter rival and eyed Khaira viciously. She completely disregarded that Noura had spent most of her formative years in this house.

Khaira ignored the woman whose arrival had sent her out of her marital home and faced her ex-husband.

"How dare you treat our daughter like this?" she demanded.

"She is no daughter of mine ..." There were deep grooves on Alhaji Kanjuni's forehead.

"At least she has a mother!" Khaira countered. "Tunde, who gave you the right to decide what is moral or not? You cannot forget that I was with you in those early days. Wallahi if anything happens to my daughter, I will scatter your secrets all over town."

Alhaji Kanjuni clenched his jaw. "You dare not."

"I will." Khaira slapped the palm of her right hand against her chest for emphasis. "You know me, I don't joke with my children." She turned to Noura. "Noura, let's go."

"If she leaves here ..." Alhaji Kanjuni's voice was grave. "If she goes refusing to denounce this nonsense she is involved in, that girl will never be welcome here. She should never step foot in this house."

"She already has a home that she is welcome in," Khaira shot over her shoulder.

***

In the Jeep, Noura could not stop the tears that fell down her face, or the way her body shook violently. It was as if she were suffering from a bout of malaria. She found a box of tissues in the back of the car and blew her nose. Khaira drove in silence. When they reached a working traffic light, she would stop to rub at her shoulders.

"Thank you ..." Noura's voice was hoarse. Yesterday and today were like nothing she had ever experienced.

Khaira only nodded curtly, her worry etched on her face. Once they reached safety within the walls of the estate, she turned off the ignition after taking down all four windows. It was only then that she started talking.

"Whatever happens, Noura, you are my daughter."

Noura lifted her feet to the seat and curled in around herself. "But you were angry with me when I told you."

"Noura, you are my daughter," Khaira repeated, and sighed. "I do not know that I can fully accept this part of you, but I know you. I brought you into this world. I loved you all these years even when your father tried to separate us. I refuse to throw my daughter away."

"But you seemed so angry in the morning," she griped.

Khaira rubbed at her closed eyelids. "That was my mistake. It was so unexpected to me that you would be a lesbian abi bisexual that I did not know how to react. As soon as I realised what you had told me, I had to do something. I contacted Taofiq and warned him to leave you alone, but in my hurry, I did not consider he would run to your father as a last resort."

"How did you know I was in the mansion?" She needed to know.

"Well," Khaira explained. "I thought I would talk to you when you came home back from work but couldn't sit still so I headed to your office believing I would catch you as you were closing so we could go for dinner somewhere. When I reached your office, I was told you had left early. I called Aida and asked her to check if you were home, and obviously, you were not there. My intuition started prickling. I had a feeling you would be at your father's house, and I knew he would react in an extreme fashion if you tried to confide in him as you did with me. Imagine threatening to send you to a *marabout*! Over my dead body."

Next, she reached for Noura's left hand and held it in a tight squeeze. "I made a mistake when I turned away from you earlier. That will be the first and the last time. I am prepared to stand by you. I am so proud of you for telling me. It must have been a hard thing for you to do. I promise to respect your wishes. You are my daughter, and I will always love you."

Fresh tears clouded her vision at her mother's words.

"I want to get to know this side of you," Khaira said. "Who is this girl you say you like? Can I meet her?"

She chuckled desolately. "That's too quick."

"It's okay." Her mother gave her hand a reassuring squeeze. "When you're ready introduce her to me, to us. We can all have dinner here. What does she like to eat?"

When they climbed out of the car, Khaira wrapped her in a tight squeeze. Noura's heart and spirit lifted—she held her mother like her life depended on it.

Later that night, she let Aida in on her reality as a woman who was in love with another woman, to her sister's shock. Before lying on the bed in the spare bedroom, she called Bewaji to let her know that the nightmare was all over.

CHAPTER TEN

Noura was going to have to leave her mother's house soon, but not just yet. She was basking in the love and affection her mother and sisters showered on her. She made plans to head to see Bewaji's now-complete mural later in the day, but for the time being, she lay in bed sending naughty messages to her lover-woman on her phone.

She was so embedded in the fantasy they had both created that she did not realise somebody was in the room until the bed sank. She lifted her head to see Rokhaya, decked in a blood red abaya and matching hijab, her makeup-less face glowing.

"Big sis," Rokhaya greeted. "How are you feeling?"

"I am fine," Noura replied, not bothering to sit up.

"How is ..." Rokhaya paused as if searching for the right words. "How is your girlfriend?"

She found herself laughing at the way her baby sister had said girlfriend, hesitant but still full of concern. It reminded her of the reason she had stayed here, of the love her sisters and mother continued to show her as they slowly came to terms with the 'new Noura.'

They were carefully treading a path that they had divorced from their reality, a subject that they had labelled as so foreign to them until Noura met Bewaji and fell for her. They had all known her to be a romantic aggressor, frequently with a boy hanging around her. She had to tell her sisters why she had become that way in the first place, to avoid a label that she felt did not apply to her in secondary school.

"She's fine." She sat up and embraced Rokhaya. "Thank you."

"What did I do?" Rokhaya held her sister. "Did I say something wrong?"

"No, you did not." She retreated, and this time sat up with her back against the headboard.

"I heard laughter." Aida appeared at the doorway holding a tray of food that she set down on the bed before Noura. She then stretched a hand and caressed the soft coils of Noura's hair. Aida smelled of Maggi, curry, and onions.

She beamed up at her sister, and then she turned her attention to the tray before her. It held a bowl of potatoes in a soup containing thin slices of beef and vegetables. There was also a cup of spiced coffee, a trademark of Khaira who loved milky coffee flavoured with cloves and at times ginger. She thanked her elder sister as Aida sat on the bed in front of her.

"Mum is minding Cheikh downstairs." Aida launched the conversation. "So you can start talking."

"Yes," Rokhaya agreed. "It is high time you tell us about her and stop dodging our questions."

"Won't I eat first?" She beamed. She had wanted to bring them in bit by bit, but her sisters clearly were tired of that strategy.

A sip of the hot coffee warmed her mouth, her throat, and between her breasts. A warmth that had more to do with the person who cooked than with the coffee itself. She took a spoonful of soup and closed her eyes, letting the flavours play in her mouth. When she opened her eyes, her sisters were staring at her, clearly impatient.

"You need to stop keeping us in suspense." Rokhaya pursed her lips.

"Please, if that's how she wants to play it." Aida cocked her eyebrows. "I am going to assume that your girlfriend is the fine babe I saw you with at that coffee shop."

A hot potato scalded Noura's tongue. She covered her mouth with a hand and blew.

"I am right, aren't I?" Aida looked over to Rokhaya. "I caught her about two months back, with one lady ... what was her name again? I can't remember. Anyway, back then, Noura obviously did not want me there. Now we all know why."

"Her name is Bewaji," she said once she'd chewed and swallowed the potato.

Aida clapped her hands in glee. "Right, Bewaji. That name suits her."

"Is she pretty?" Rokhaya asked.

"Yes," Aida and Noura chorused.

She giggled when Aida launched into a poetic description of Bewaji's physical beauty.

"She is a tall, fair babe with a Fulani nose. When I shook her hand, it felt as soft a butter. That girl's shape ehn …"

"Stop!" Noura protested, chuckling.

"Do you really love her?" Rokhaya asked in an excited tone.

Aida opened her mouth and closed it almost instantly. Noura could easily guess the words that were on the tip of her elder sister's tongue, "*of course she does!*" But Aida waited for her to say the words herself.

"I mean, I like her a lot." She ate some more. "And when I tried to stay away from her because I thought my feelings were wrong, I realised I did not want to be without her."

"Ra-ra is avoiding the L-word." Aida gloated.

"Okay, I'll talk." She glanced from Aida to Rokhaya then back. "When I first saw Bewaji, I felt a sudden, very intense attraction. Aida, you remember when you said love would hit me like a slap in the face?"

Her sister beamed as she inclined her head.

"I felt like my whole universe tilted," she went on. "It took a while for me to finally admit that I am attracted to Bewaji. That I am in love with a woman. I am feeling this love like I never even dreamed of before."

There was silence in the room as her sisters took in what she said. She ate her rapidly cooling food and sniffed because the ata rodo in the soup made her eyes water. Already, the thump of her heart danced to Bewaji's tune.

"Does she know?" Rokhaya asked from her quiet corner.

"I think she does," Noura said. "If not, she will soon. I'm seeing her this evening."

***

Danjuma needed to hurry up and leave. Bewaji stilled her left foot from tapping. She harshly reminded herself that she needed to be professional, but Noura would be here soon, and she still hadn't set things up.

"Did you get my email?" he asked as he bent forward to examine her recently completed mural.

She answered affirmatively. As part of the pre-opening publicity for the restaurant, DJ and Loreen wanted to have her interviewed by a popular blogger.

"Great. I'll go ahead and set things up for next week," he said. "Thanks for agreeing to it."

She nodded absentmindedly. She had already decided that by doing the interview, she would also be creating exposure for her work. Now that she was done here, she would be technically jobless until the next client waltzed in.

"Did you hear anything I just said?" He eyed her.

She had not even been aware that he was talking. "Of course, sir."

He tilted his head.

"Don't *sir* me," he said, then his phone rang.

Saved by the ringtone, she glanced at the watch on her left wrist then at the door.

"I have to leave now, Bewaji," he announced. "Thanks for agreeing to do the interview. I will get back to you on the details later."

Danjuma rushed out the front door so quickly that he did not see her Cheshire cat grin. As the door shut behind him, she rushed upstairs to complete the final details of her surprise for Noura.

She lit scented candles and placed them in strategic locations around the room, then unrolled the soft carpet she had brought from home. The next thing was to call the delivery man and demand to know why the food she'd ordered over an hour ago had yet to arrive. She had champagne in a cooler and the highlife Noura liked so much playing softly in the background. She checked her phone again, counting down the seconds until Noura arrived.

She waited by the front door after the delivery man finally reached her destination. She toyed with one of her smaller brushes, twirling in between her fingers in her impatience. Dusk fell before Noura's car drove in.

"So sorry I am late." Noura rushed to throw her arms around her waist. "Traffic was serious."

As had become usual, Bewaji's body warmed up at her touch. She waved away the apology.

"Let's go upstairs." She tugged at her hand.

"Hold on." Noura looked puzzled. "Let's see your warrior woman mural. I thought that's what I'm here for."

Noura moved inch-by-inch studying the mural, taking far too much time for Bewaji. It told the story of a huntress, showing scenes from her adventure through the savannah and later in an underwater kingdom. She had wanted to link this mural with the one upstairs and chose to make the woman in the lake a recurring figure. Presently, Noura lingered in front of a scene that depicted the huntress kneeling before the lake in conversation with the mysterious woman in the water.

"Are you sure this woman is not me?" She squinted at the mural. "I mean, the one in the lake."

"No, she isn't."

"But she has my nose-ring and everything," Noura protested.

"Okay, fine, she's you."

"I knew it!" Noura was triumphant. "And I bet the huntress is you. She has your hair."

"Those are supposed to be dreadlocks," she pointed out.

"Whatever. So are the huntress and the woman in the lake lovers?" Noura asked, dragging the conversation even further.

Groaning with impatience, she wrapped her arms around Noura's waist and held her close. She kissed the curve of her neck, a spot that she knew held Noura's weakness. Sure enough, Noura stopped laughing in celebration of her win and shuddered.

"I have a surprise for you," she whispered. "Let's go upstairs."

This time, there was no hesitation. Holding her hand in hers, Bewaji led her upstairs. Noura gasped at the display.

"This is beautiful, baby." She cupped Bewaji's face in her hands and placed a quick peck on her lips. "What's for dinner?"

"Chinese."

Noura squealed, then rushed to the small carpet and picked the bunch of flowers she had ordered. There were roses, dahlias, and cosmos wrapped in a coloured paper.

"No one has bought me flowers before." She chuckled.

They rushed through dinner and afterwards cuddled. Bewaji lay on her back, one arm wrapped around Noura, who kept her head on her shoulder. As she held on to Noura's soft body, she traced her fingers in lazy patterns over her back. She could feel the smooth skin below the thin fabric of the boubou Noura wore.

"Why did you decide to tell your parents about me after you had denied it?" She intertwined her fingers with Noura's. They were reminiscing on the Taofiq episode.

"I did not want Taofiq, or anyone like him, for that matter, holding that over me," Noura explained. She slipped a hand under Bewaji's tank top and caressed her flat tummy. "And I also realised that loving you will never be a sin."

"Does your friend still plan on having Taofiq assaulted?" she wondered out loud.

Noura laughed—she had thought Gigi was joking, but the woman had been dead serious. While Gigi was relieved that she was fine and well after Taofiq's attempt at blackmail, she was still ready to make good on her earlier threat.

"I talked her out of it. She's taking me out this weekend to celebrate my metamorphosis into a woman who loves another woman."

"Loves?" Bewaji tickled Noura's side. "You did not tell me anything about love, unless there's really another woman."

Noura shifted her face and looked into her eyes.

"I love you, Bewaji," she professed. "And I want to fall even deeper in love with you. I want to hold you and make love to you. I want to kiss your lips first thing in the morning and give you back rubs at night."

It was true that despite the relatively short period, Noura was in love. A love that was more intense than anything she had ever felt before. She took in the instant way her body had reacted to Bewaji at first sight and the way her mind and heart unfurled down the line.

Bewaji, meanwhile, beamed from ear to ear. She pushed Noura on her back and looked down on her love's upturned face. She planted a light kiss on Noura's forehead, then on the bridge of her nose, then finally on her eager lips.

"I want all that and more with you, too, Noura," she whispered against her ear.

THE END

Thank you for reading A Little Bit of Love's Magic by Bambo Deen.

If you enjoyed this story, please leave a review on the site of purchase.

Continue reading for an excerpt from Daemon Trapped by Bambo Deen featured in the Enchanted Anthology: Volume Two.

BLURB

When long-suffering daemon Leonidas is trapped in Besidas' hotel, she is drawn into a world of curious and strange creatures. Stranded after a cruel attempt on his life, Leon has spent decades trying and failing to return home. Besi evokes emotions within him that he did not think were possible for his kind and for the first time he's enjoying Earth. But can Leon protect Besi when a dangerous entity from Leon's past comes for revenge?

EXCERPT from *Daemon Trapped* by **Bambo Deen**

PROLOGUE

The Forest had appointed four guards to preside over the four entrances that led to the home of different kinds of daemons and all sorts of creatures—both good and evil.

One day, the Western Guard fell into a trap specially set for him. What had started as a stroll to his post from his home ended with him looking up at the sky from a hole deep in the earth. He had not seen it coming.

He landed in the trap with his tools, his wand—a wooden figurine crafted for him by the Forest itself—in his hand. He could fly out of the hole with its help. However, with each attempt at escape, he felt the power of his life force draining out from him.

Truly in a bind, he had no other choice but to call for help. He screamed 'til his throat was sore.

When the familiar face of the Southern

Guard appeared above him, relief flooded through him.

"Help me out of here," he called up.

To his surprise, the Southern Guard sneered. "Since you love humans so much, why don't you live among them?"

The Southern Guard waved his own wand, and the earth started shaking. The loose dirt beneath the Western Guard's feet slipped.

"The Forest pardoned me," the Western Guard shouted, but his colleague had disappeared.

His legs sank deeper into the hole, and glancing down, he saw what looked like another sky opening up below him.

He fell through the hole that became the sky and landed with a earth-shattering crash.

CHAPTER ONE

Besida Agbajor wasn't one for late nights in the office. But with her new bosses currently on vacation in Samoa during the week of their scheduled monthly meetings, she had little choice. She tilted her right ear to meet her shoulder as she scanned through the financials again.

"They aren't going to like this," she said to her empty office.

She had set jazz to play over the speakers an hour ago, and it did nothing to calm her nerves. She abruptly stopped the music and pushed her swivel chair away from her desk and laptop.

Rising to her bare feet—she had kicked off her heels a while back—she walked towards the window. Through the firmly shut sliding glass windows and the insect-proof netting, she counted three cars in parking lot of Gazania Hotels. The crowd that had stormed through the doors following the drama two weeks ago was thinning out.

Besi had to admit to herself that she had

done a poor job of containing that scandal involving the former governor turned senator's wife and her lovers. After a blogger had put photos of the location online in a post that painted their establishment as a den of orgies, things had worsened. Gazania promised a secluded, private environment for anyone looking for a mindful retreat, so seeing their name and address plastered all over the Internet had been a huge blow.

Closing her eyes, she inhaled deeply. She held that breath for a beat and then let it go, imagining all her nervousness slipping away. Her laptop started dinging behind her, letting her know a call was coming through.

She squared her shoulders as she spun and returned to her desk. Somehow, it was less nerve-racking managing millions of dollars for seed companies than it was managing just one branch of her parents' business.

"Good evening," she greeted her parents.

William and Lolade Agbajor were seated in what could have been a generic room if not for the azure waters glimpsed from the open windows behind them.

"Good evening, Besi," Lolade replied. "We've had a chance to look through the files you sent last night."

It would have been surprising but not

unwelcome if her parents had started with small talk about her personal life. Besi had not spoken to them outside business in months. Still, she went full swing into the details they required. In the middle of expounding on the figures from the recently opened pan-Asian restaurant that had been her idea, a small knock came on the door.

She glanced up—she had given express instructions not to be disturbed.

"As I was saying ..." she attempted to continue.

The knocking stopped, but now, her phone started vibrating loudly against the wooden surface of her desk.

She shot a quick look at her phone— Miranda, her operations manager who should know better than to disturb her. She hit the red button.

"Don't you want to answer that?" William asked.

"Not right now," she replied, shifting in her chair. Her phone began vibrating again. "It's from the hotel ..."

"And you would ignore it?" Lolade's voice dripped with disapproval.

Besi groaned inwardly at yet another faux pas.

"Excuse me then," she said and hastily rescheduled the call before calling Miranda.

"Hello, Miranda." She tried her best not to sound irritated.

"Sorry to disturb you, ma," Miranda said, clearly excited. "I am outside your office."

"Come in," she said before hanging up.

From the door, she immediately sensed something was up. Miranda rushed in, and when she was close enough, Besi saw her eyes were sparkling.

"What's the matter?"

"We have another situation." Miranda had whispered the last word.

"A what?" Besi jumped to her feet.

"Like the one with the senator's wife." Miranda let the implication hang in the air.

Cold dread washed over Besi, and she fell back into her chair.

"How bad is it? Who knows?"

"No one but me," Miranda replied confidently. "I heard someone shouting for help and rushed to investigate."

"You're sure no one heard this?" Besi asked again. She looked at her laptop to confirm its lid was down.

"I'm sure. You said it before, 'Don't raise any alarm, don't let anyone know that anything is out of the ordinary'."

"Great job, Miranda. Let's go."

Besi followed Miranda out her office. The

door creaked closed behind them as they walked down the hallway. She was only a couple of months into this position and this town, so on any given day, she made sure she took the time out to appreciate the fact that this building was built in the colonial style.

Years ago when she had still been in New York, her parents had bought and transformed the house into this ten-room boutique hotel. However, as Miranda continued sharing the sparing details she knew of the current situation, Besi's entire body thrummed with impatience. Several images of what could have gone wrong swiped through her mind.

By the time they reached the door of the double room in the eastern wing, her stomach was rolling.

***

Leonidas' arms hurt, suspended as they were above his head, held in place by a pair of fluffy pink handcuffs. He shifted to lean his head, pressing it against the cool, tiled bathroom wall.

On any other day, he'd admire the details reminiscent of a Moroccan hammam. Frankly, every detail about this hotel had stood out to him from as early as when he'd driven past the gates artfully shielded with creeping vines. He would have savoured every detail if he hadn't been accosted in such an unseemly manner.

For the umpteenth time, he'd been bested. When he thought about it, this was less dangerous than other situations he had been in. Handcuffed to the shower in a fancy hotel, mostly naked. Becca and Razaq had taken pictures before they had left him, and Leon imagined those images would soon be online somewhere. What would the headlines say? Now that he couldn't picture, thanks to Rike—everything that came up on the Internet about him boasted about his brilliance and success.

"*The brilliant woodworker bringing life to the homes of celebrities*"

"*We are collectively swooning over Leonidas Okpe*"

"*30 under 30: The designer, Leonidas Okpe*"

The last one made him chuckle. *30 under 30* indeed—he had way more years than that under his belt.

He held back a yelp as his back muscles clamped down hard. He had done enough of that to know help was on the way. He gazed at the key resting on the edge of the washbasin.

Levitating was out of the question; that had never been his speciality. He had tried to disappear and will himself back home, but that had been unsuccessful. His energy levels were low, and after spending hours in this situation, he now suspected he had been drugged. He knew betrayal intimately, but at least, Becca and Razaq hadn't tried to kill him and inadvertently sent him to another universe. He shook his head and let it hang heavy, waiting for help.

"Excuse me," a soft voice drifted from the bathroom door. "Good evening, I am Besi Agbajor, General Manager of Gazania."

"Good evening," he grunted in reply.

"I'll be coming in now," she announced.

It sounded like she was struggling to get the door open. He heard one push and then another before the door gave way. His head swam at the sight of Besi, and he was immediately drawn to her angelic eyes set in a heart-shaped face accentuated by long braids. She was stunning.

***

Besi gasped. The first thing she saw was the broad expanse of his chest emphasised by the thick, strong arms that were suspended. His hips were lean in his black boxers that didn't leave anything to the imagination. She had never read *Fifty Shades of Grey*, but something about this bound man sent shivers straight between her legs.

He sent a lopsided smile at her, and goose bumps broke over her skin.

"The keys are on the basin," he said, pointing with his chin.

Those words snapped her out of whatever

the hell that had been. She squared her shoulders and looked at the direction he indicated. Whoever had cuffed him there had left the keys.

A thousand and one questions ran through her mind, but the man looked tired, his face pale and drawn. She grabbed the keys and approached the bathtub. She looked up—she wasn't short, but she would need to tap into her yoga lessons to reach the shower head he was anchored to.

"Excuse me." She lifted one leg then the other to the rim of the bathtub, and she now stood face to face with him, looking into his eyes.

Besi swayed slightly. She looked up and scolded herself into concentration. Stretching one arm up, she sought the handcuffs with the keys. The other hand held the rail as she tried to insert the key into the tiny lock. She could feel the heat of his body and the light flutter of his breath. The lock resisted before giving way, and just as it clicked, she slipped.

It was a short fall, wouldn't have been anything serious if she had tipped backwards. But she'd slipped forward, her body gliding against the man she had just freed. She felt his arms try to hold her and fail. Embarrassment coursed through her veins, and it took all of her pride to hold her head high as she stepped out of the tub and away from him.

"Thank you," he said, stepping out of the tub, too. "This feels good, I ..."

She reached out as the man swayed on his feet. His weight strained on her, and she called over to Miranda for help. Together, they placed him on the bed.

"Do we need a doctor?" Miranda worried her bottom lip.

"Probably." Besi looked down at him. "Who knows how long he's been hanging there."

"But which doctor will come at this time? What if he dies? You know who he is, don't you?"

"Not going to happen," she hushed Miranda. "I think I can call someone."

In her haste to get here, she had left her phone in her office. She rushed towards the door, but his voice stopped her. As she looked over her shoulder, her eyes widened at the sight of him sitting up. He was calmly wearing his clothes as if he had not been in handcuffs for hours. As if he had no lost consciousness.

"Excuse me, Mister ..." she started.

"Just call me Leon," he said, before clearing his throat. "There is no need for a doctor."

"Are you sure you're all right?" She had to search through her brain for the appropriate words.

"I am," he replied, and incredulously, he winked at her. "I can't find my phone. Is there any

I can borrow?"

"Mine," Miranda said, her phone in her hands.

Besi waited until Miranda had made the call to Leon's personal assistant and then entered Boss mode. The panic at not knowing what was going on in her hotel had dissipated.

"Miranda, do you mind excusing us?" she said.

Once Miranda was gone, she glared at Leon. He was fully dressed now, in tailored pants and a collared shirt, looking more like a distinguished businessman than anything else.

"I know you've had a tough time," she began. "But Mr. Leon, can you please tell me what happened? I need to be ready for any backlash. I'm sure you understand."

"Just Leon," he replied.

He was wearing cufflinks now. Once he was done, he turned to face her, and once again, she was drawn to his eyes.

"I am terribly sorry that this happened at your establishment—which is an outstanding one, I must say. What happened here was a childish prank gone wrong, but still a prank nonetheless. I came here with friends and will be meeting them shortly after I leave. I promise that your hotel won't appear in the gossip rags."

Besi found herself nodding at everything he said. His words were calm and measured; he weighed everything before speaking as a shopper would select the best fruit at the market.

"There is really no reason to worry," he repeated. "My assistant will soon be here."

"All right," she said. "I'll be outside if you need anything."

It was after she had returned to her office that she realised that he hadn't really told her anything.

***

Free at last, Leon thought. Even though he was still bound in other ways. Like to this world, for one. He slipped into his shoes and stole another glance at the owner of the hotel as she walked away. He shook his head. Now was not the time to dwell on how beautiful his rescuer was.

When he thought of it, the last woman who had saved him had been bewitching, too. A human who had wandered so deep into the wooded forests that she had ended up in his world of daemons— varied spirits, wraiths, strange and curious creatures; Forest Home.

This had happened at least a hundred years ago if one was going by time as the humans today calculated it, but Leon recalled it as if it were yesterday. He could see her face peering down the hole he had been trapped in and left to die. Forest Home was a dangerous place, even for those that lived it in.

Several sharpened wooden stakes had pierced through his body, the pain rendering him witless, and she had saved him with his own magic. To repay his debt to her, he had looked the other way and let her roam Forest Home; a place that was forbidden to humans and had four guards to ensure this rule was maintained.

That one action would irrevocably change his life. Just his bad luck that the next time he had been dropped into a hole, she hadn't been there to save him. Nonetheless, she was still the reason he was free and thriving.

The door creaked open, and Rike, his assistant barged in. She looked so much like her ancestor, the adventurous huntress who had saved him and now left him in the care of her descendants.

"Who was it this time?" she demanded, crossing her arms over her chest. "I keep telling you not to trust people knowing your propensity for getting betrayed."

Rike was always protective of him, which he found funny at times because she wasn't the supernatural being in this situation.

"It was Becca and Razaq. They seem to have taken my phone, too."

"Damn it," she cursed. She eyed him from his head to his feet, her concern evident in her eyes. "Should I hex them? I will hex them."

"No need." He tapped her on her shoulder. "Let's go home for now."

***

In his study, Leon settled heavily on the oversized leather chair. It was strategically placed in front of the window that offered a stunning view of his garden, but this late at night, the view was blocked by thick velvet curtains. He removed his cufflinks and placed them on the ebony accent table before leaning even deeper into the chair.

"You know they just called me to ask if I was available," Leon said. "I had no suspicion ..."

"I say this with all my love," Rike replied as she picked up his cufflinks. "But you never have any idea."

He groaned. "They took pictures of me! In a very indecent state."

"I'll sort that out, don't worry." She walked over to the mini-bar on the other side of the room, next to the desk. "You're not going to end up on the Internet."

"Thank you, Rike." He accepted the glass of aged whiskey she handed to him and downed the drink in one gulp.

"While we're on the topic, I have an update

on what we've been looking for," Rike said as she refilled his glass.

When Leon had found himself in this world, it had been Rike's grandmother who had saved him. But his relationship with the family stretched even further back—aeons ago, her ancestor had saved him in the Forest Home.

On this side, he happily entered a contract with the Folahan family where they managed his wealth and provided him a cover for his apparent immortality. Rike was different from her predecessors—she'd come in four years ago and surprised him with her multiple piercings, tattoos, and bleached Afro. He had initially assumed a young woman like her would not be interested in taking over the family business, but Rike was well-versed in the tradition of magic that had been passed down from her mothers. She was also more than happy to modernise the relationship her family had with Leon.

She was the reason his architecture hobby had become beloved by the crème de la crème of Nigerian society. She was the reason he'd made it to the headlines. He liked laying low and wanted to keep it that way, but Rike had other plans. She wanted him to leave with a bang, as she put it, because she was sure she would be the one to help him return to the Forest.

"Fuck it," she'd said. "You're going to be out of this world soon. Just go large then go home."

True to her word, she was good at making things happen. Now thanks to her, they had the first lead to getting him back home that he had come across in decades.

"I have established contact with the seller," she was saying as she swiped through her tablet. "And I'm this close to placing the order. The seller is saying it'll take a couple of weeks to reach Nigeria."

"We don't have weeks," he started, then grinned at the absurdity of that statement. Both of them knew that he had been trying to find the wand—the emblem of his power that had gone missing when he'd landed here—for a very long time. "Travel to wherever is nearest to the seller and take the next flight back."

"I've always wanted to go to the Bahamas," she said, a lopsided grin on her face.

He narrowed his eyes even though he was smiling.

"All right, okay," Rike launched. "I'll go to New York tomorrow ... I mean, later today ... and be back before you know it."

"Great." He nodded.

He would not think about how his wand had found its way across the ocean. To the person who was selling it online, it was an authentic African antique belonging to the Yoruba people of southwestern Nigeria. To Leon, it was a personal treasure not of this world, not only a one-of-a-kind gift made for him by the Forest, but intimately tied to his duty as a guard.

From the few daemons that had come to Earth after him, he'd learned that the Forest had gone into disarray since its Western Guard had disappeared. With such an imbalance, the already violent place became more precarious as the more evil forest creatures multiplied and wreaked havoc on the peace-loving ones.

It didn't matter that he was now buying back his own property or that it had been stolen from him initially, even before he could have figured out how to create a portal leading back home. Before, it wouldn't have occurred to him to check the websites Rike knew of. And this statue looked so much like his wand, the only way to know for sure would be to hold it in his hands. It was imperative that he return home.

"Let me call the travel agent," Rike announced, already on her way out the study.

"Before you go," he said just as she was about to open the door. "Kindly order for some flowers sent to Gazania."

The thought had swept through his mind,

and he'd grabbed it. He had just met Besi Agbajor, but he'd felt a connection he wanted to pursue, and not because he had a thing for human women saving him from trouble.

Rike paused, brow raised. "The hotel? Who should the flowers be addressed to?"

"The manager," he replied, trying to keep a poker face. "What? I'm just extending my thanks for her cool-headed resolution of an embarrassing situation."

She did not say anything, but Leon could feel her gaze boring into him. Sometimes, he swore she used her magic to make it feel like the back of his neck was on fire.

He shifted in the chair and finally looked over his shoulder to where she stood by the door.

Finally, she spoke. "What's up? Are you trying to set yourself for another betrayal? You could die this time."

"Like I said," he repeated. "I'm expressing my thanks. She saved me."

"Sure," she said, rolling her eyes. "You never listen to me anyway."

Leon heard her murmuring about how she would still have to clean up after him before she could close the door behind her.

OTHER BOOKS BY LOVE AFRICA PRESS

Enchanted: Volume Two Anthology

Queer and Sexy Collection by Eniitan

Bound to Liberty by Kiru Taye

Revelations by Lauri Kubuitsile

Fine Maple by Emem Bassey

CONNECT WITH US

Facebook.com/LoveAfricaPress

Twitter.com/LoveAfricaPress

Instagram.com/LoveAfricaPress

www.loveafricapress.com

LOVE AFRICA
PRESS
African Love Stories